SOLITUDES, GALLERIES *and other poems*

SOLITUDES,

Antonio Machado

GALLERIES *and other poems*

Translated by Richard L. Predmore

With an Introduction by Michael P. Predmore

Duke University Press
Durham   1987

Publication of this book was supported by the Program for Cultural Cooperation Between Spain's Ministry of Culture and United States' Universities.

The Spanish text of *Soledades, galerías y otros poemas* printed in this edition is from Antonio Machado, *Poesías completas*, 1936. Reprinted by permission of Dr. José Rollán Riesco, legal representative of the heirs of Antonio Machado.

Library of Congress Cataloging-in-Publication Data
Machado, Antonio, 1875–1939.
Solitudes, galleries, and other poems.
Spanish text, parallel English translation of:
Soledades, galerías, otros poemas.
Bibliography: p.
I. Title.
PQ 6623.A3A26   1987   861'.62   86-32758
ISBN 0-8223-0713-8

✳ CONTENTS

GALERÍAS • GALLERIES

VARIA • VARIA

✳ TRANSLATOR'S PREFACE

In the postscript to his history of Spanish literature, Gerald Brenan reviews the achievements of Spanish letters in the light of an implied comparison with English and European literature. He concludes that in poetry, particularly lyric poetry, Spain enjoys a preeminence with which only the English can compete. Coming down to the twentieth century, he asserts that "Antonio Machado and García Lorca rank in power and genius with the finest poets of this century."[1] And this is not an isolated opinion. Waldo Frank has written that at the outset of the Spanish Civil War Antonio Machado had come to be regarded as the first poet of Spain.[2] More recently, a supremely gifted poet and respected professor, Jorge Guillén, did not hesitate to affirm that Antonio Machado is simply the best poet of the century.[3] Needless to say, not all competent critics would place Machado quite so high as the three I have just quoted, but there can be no doubt that his place among the major poets of his country is assured.

Despite his stature, none of the poet's books has been translated to English in its entirety. Several well-known translators have translated selected poems, but in no case are they extensive enough to provide an adequate basis for attempting the interpretation of a whole work. I have undertaken a complete translation of *Soledades, galerías y otros poemas*,[4] partly because of its intrinsic value and partly because it is a landmark not only in the evolution of Machado's own poetry but also in the introduction of Symbolism into the mainstream of twentieth-century Spanish poetry.

In order to help the reader to understand what I have tried to do, I

1

must recall a few of the obvious problems faced by translators. Everybody knows that it is very difficult to translate poetry from one language to another. In the best of cases, something is always lost. Recognizing this, some translators strive for what have been called "reënactments." Their point of departure is a specific poem, but in their version of it they show more interest in creating an attractive poem than in being faithful to the sense of the original. There may be nothing wrong with this, so long as the reader is permitted to know that the translation doesn't pretend to be an accurate rendition of the original. If the translator is poetically endowed, his translation may have much aesthetic merit.

Then there are translators more interested in conveying the exact sense of a poem than in recreating the perfection of its form. But even these translators do not ordinarily renounce the hope of retaining as much of the formal beauty of the original as possible. In the end, most translators have to be satisfied with some sort of compromise between the extremes of formless literalness and free reënactments. One can only classify himself, then, somewhere along this continuum. For myself, I must say that I have struggled hardest to preserve the sense of the original.[5]

To be more specific, I have renounced the attempt to re-create faithfully the metrical patterns of the originals. Such an attempt would probably have led me into numerous betrayals of sense and to little success in the imitation of verse forms. I have tried to avoid using fancy language to translate what Machado has expressed in plain language. Where he repeats a word in the same stanza or brief poem, I do the same on the assumption that he meant to do what he did. I have intended to translate the most frequently used words in his diction consistently enough to enable the reader to recognize the possibility that they are key elements in a symbolic system that could not be sustained in English if they were translated to accommodate only their immediate context.

There is no doubt that a symbolic system is at work in *Soledades, galerías y otros poemas*, a system essential to full understanding of these poems and impossible to appreciate in a translation that took very many liberties with its key structural elements. Taking this system fully into account, Professor M. P. Predmore has developed a

2

coherent interpretation of *Soledades, galerías y otros poemas*. It is based on long and detailed study of the Spanish text. I have asked him to write an introduction incorporating a brief version of his interpretation supported by quotations from my translation. I find his interpretation convincing. I leave it to the reader to judge whether the quotations from my translation convincingly support that interpretation.

The Spanish text that I have translated is essentially the version of *Soledades, galerías y otros poemas* that appears in the last edition of Machado's *Poesías completas* to be published in his lifetime.[6] I have compared this text with such other editions as I have been able to lay my hands on. The most useful of these is that of Geoffrey Ribbans,[7] who has been able to consult all of the primary editions and also the excellent critical edition of Oreste Macrí.[8] In the end, however, I have chosen to respect the edition that we must assume comes closest to representing the will of the poet, that is, the text of the 1936 edition of his *Poesías completas*. I have limited my changes to a few matters of punctuation and to an occasional obvious misprint like *preclamo* for *preclaro* in poem LXXXIX or an errant preposition and article as in "el patio *del* silencioso" in poem VII.

R. L. Predmore
Durham, N.C.

Notes

1 Gerald Brenan, *The Literature of the Spanish People* (New York: Meridian Books, 1957), p. 457.

2 *Repertorio Americano*, Costa Rica (22 April 1939), p. 56. Reproduced in *Antonio Machado: El escritor y la crítica*, ed. Ricardo Gullón and Allen W. Phillips (Madrid: Taurus, 1973).

3 "Más allá del soliloquio," *Poesía*. Revista ilustrada de información poética, Ministerio de Cultura, Madrid, 17 (Primavera 1983), p. 19.

4 Antonio Machado's first published collection of poems is called *Soledades* (Madrid: Imprenta de A. Álvarez, 1903). It contains only forty-two poems. What Machado called the second edition of this work was expanded to contain ninety-three poems under the title of *Soledades. Galerías. Otros poemas* (Madrid: Librería de Pueyo, 1907). Poems now numbered LIX, LX and LXXXVI were added in the 1917 edition of *Poesías completas*. Poem LXVI was added in the 1936 edition of *Poesías completas*, and this completes the canon of what is now generally accepted as Machado's first major collection of poems.

3

I have chosen to write *Soledades, galerías y otros poemas* with commas rather than with periods for three reasons: the last two times Machado is known to have written the title he used commas (in prologues dated in 1917 and 1919; see Ribbans, pp. 272–73), most scholars and critics refer to it in that form, and that is the form that best suggests the unity of the work.

5 I like to think that Antonio Machado might have approved of this decision. In the Prologue to his *Páginas escogidas* (1917), after calling Rubén Darío "the matchless master of form and sensation," he writes: "But I sought . . . to follow a very different path. I thought the poetic element was not the word valued for its sound, nor color, nor line, nor a complex of sensations, but a deep palpitation of the spirit; what the soul contributes, if it contributes anything, or what it says, if it says anything, with its own voice, in animated response to contact with the world."

6 *Poesías completas* (Madrid: Espasa-Calpe, 1936).

7 Antonio Machado, *Soledades. Galerías. Otros poemas*, ed. Geoffrey Ribbans (Madrid: Cátedra, 1983).

8 *Poesie, studi introduttivi, testo criticamente riveduto, traduzione, note al testo, commento, bibliografia*, 3rd ed. (Milan: Lerici, 1969).

✳ INTRODUCTION

A towering figure in the literature and culture of twentieth-century
Spain, Antonio Machado is considered by many contemporary poets
and critics of his country as the most important Spanish poet of this
century. He constitutes, together with his contemporary, Juan Ramón
Jiménez, one of the two most important and powerful influences on the
development of what later becomes the most brilliant flowering of Eu-
ropean lyric poetry since the Spanish Golden Age. Machado, even
before Jiménez, introduced in his *Soledades, galerías y otros poemas*
(1898–1907) a new mode of poetic composition—a new mode of sym-
bolic poetry—to Spanish letters. In this brief but essential work, one
can note already the beginnings of a poetic consciousness and vision
that will reach in the poet's later work of the 1920s and 1930s a level
of historical and social awareness superior to that of any other Spanish
writer of the first three generations of this century.

In aspects of both form and content, therefore, *Soledades, galerías
y otros poemas* is certainly a key point of departure for serious stu-
dents of twentieth-century Spanish poetry.

Life

Antonio Machado was born in Seville in 1875 and died in exile in
Southern France in 1939. He spent his childhood and young manhood
in Seville and Madrid. Active as both poet and writer for over thirty
years, he also pursued a career in teaching and spent the greater part
of his adult life as a professor of French in the Institutes of Soria,

5

Baeza, and Segovia. In other words, he passed most of his professional career as a high school teacher of French in the small provincial cities of rural Spain, in Castile, and upper Andalusia. It is of special importance, I think, to note that both his family and education were formative influences in his early development. His father and grandfather were prominent intellectual and politically active figures of their time.

His grandfather occupied a chair of natural history at the University of Seville and later became rector of the same university. During the revolutionary period of 1868–74, he played an important role as member of the revolutionary junta in Seville, and later as governor of the province. Machado's father earned a law degree at the University of Seville, but he soon abandoned a law career in favor of investigations in the field of Spanish folklore, where he achieved high distinction. Indeed, he was in his time and is today considered a pioneer in this field, one of the founders of folkloric studies in Spain. His scholarly talents were matched as well by his republican fervor, and he devoted a great deal of his time to journalism and to propagandistic activity against the injustices and corruption of the Restoration Monarchy (1875–1931), which had been reinstituted after the overthrow of the First Spanish Republic (1873). In fact, so outspoken was he in his anticlericalism and so strong in his opposition to the prevailing political climate that he seriously jeopardized his professional career.

Turning briefly to Machado's early education, we note that his first remembered and most beloved teacher, Francisco Giner de los Ríos, was the greatest educator of three generations of Spaniards. After the failure of the First Republic and the restoration of the Bourbon monarchy, a small group of dedicated idealists, headed by Giner, set themselves the task of reforming the educational and cultural life of the country. They founded in Madrid in 1876 the Free Institution for Education (*Institución Libre de Enseñanza*), which was privately funded and relatively free of the influence of church and state. Ideally, the goal of Giner and his friends was to create an intellectual and moral elite, whose influence was to multiply over the years, as a means of preparing a better climate out of which a better politics—a democratic republic—was to emerge. The historian Raymond Carr says of this in-

6

stitution that "it represented the most serious and consistent attempt to create the intellectual preconditions of a liberal democracy." [1]

At its inception, the institution devoted itself especially to primary and secondary education. Machado entered its primary school at the age of eight. In fact, the entire Machado family was always close to Giner's institution and its circle of friends and supporters. Both in Seville and Madrid, the family maintained close ties with the most liberal and progressive members of their middle-class society. Indeed, among their friends numbered two of the most dedicated and prominent Republican political figures of the time: Francisco Pi y Margall and Nicolás Salmerón, both of 'whom served as presidents of the First Spanish Republic. Machado, on more than one occasion, was to acknowledge the value of the education he received and the lessons of history and politics he learned from men such as these. This climate, then, of both political and educational reform, of opposition to the dominance of the ruling oligarchy (which reinstituted the corrupt monarchy), was to leave its profound stamp upon the poet throughout the rest of his life. The defeat of the First Republic, the return of the Bourbon monarchy, the ethical and civic fervor of a group of reform-minded idealists—these social and historical circumstances constitute something of the essential background of Antonio Machado. As we have seen, his grandfather participated in the First Spanish Republic; he himself participated until the very end in the defense of the Second Spanish Republic (1931–39). Thus, through his family, teachers and friends, and through his own conduct and activity, we see the tradition and practice of republicanism as a distinguishing characteristic.

I intend to suggest during the course of this introduction how something of the liberal and democratic ideals of his family and teachers make their way into his early lyric poetry.

Soledades, galerías y otros poemas:
Its Significance and Historical Importance

One of the strongest impressions of Machado's poetry is the enduring sense of profundity and unity we receive from so small a work. Three slender volumes—*Soledades, galerías y otros poemas* (1898–1907), *Campos de Castilla* (1907–17), and *Nuevas canciones* (1917–24)—constitute the first three books to appear. Thereafter, Machado simply added new sections, such as the "Cancionero apócrifo" ("Apocryphal Song Book"), or expanded earlier works, such as *Nuevas canciones*, and included them in successive editions (1917, 1928, 1933, 1936) of his *Poesías completas.*[2]

Soledades, the first masterpiece of this brief but essential opus, is the cornerstone of Machado's entire literary production, which, in addition to the complete poems, includes a few hundred pages of philosophical prose and six plays, written in collaboration with his brother Manuel. The personal, intimate poetry of *Soledades*, invested nonetheless with social and historical sensitivity, prepares us for the socially committed poetry of *Campos de Castilla*. And, of special interest to our present study, the influence of traditional forms of folk poetry in *Soledades* continues in the ballad, "La tierra de Alvargonzález," and in the "Proverbios y cantares" of *Campos de Castilla*; becomes the primary inspiration in the *coplas* and *soleares* of *Nuevas canciones*; and reappears again in his plays, especially in *La Lola se va a los puertos*, 1929 (*Lola Goes Off to the Ports*). Recently Alan Trueblood has well observed of *Nuevas Canciones* that "the increased prominence . . . of compositions in which the poet's individual voice seeks attunement to the collective voice of popular poetry, Andalusian or Castilian, is symptomatic of a continuing search for forms of expression facilitating communion with others. . . ."[3] Indeed, Machado's interest in and respect for folk wisdom becomes a major theme of the brilliant prose (1934–36) of the "apocryphal professor," Juan de Mairena, as he seeks to dignify the concept of popular culture and to incorporate its knowledge and wisdom into Spanish national life. In fact, various facets of both form and content of Machado's earliest work radiate out and nurture nearly all aspects of the poet's subsequent production. Antonio Sánchez-Barbudo put the matter well when he commented on the profound relationship between the beginning and the end of Machado's literary trajectory: "In his final years, Machado, the philosopher, would do no more than meditate on the experience of the young poet of *Soledades*."[4]

Perhaps there is no better example of the profundity and unity of

Machado's artistic inspiration than that provided by a single recurring image, the image of a loved one, a Persephone figure, central to the traveler's quest in *Soledades*. Anticipating for a moment the fuller consideration of Persephone in the next section of the introduction, we may say that this lovely and tragic figure exercises a powerful and permanent grip on the poet's imagination. She is introduced as the "elusive virgin ever by my side" (poems XVI and XXIX) in *Soledades* and undergoes a variety of transformations, appearing most notably as Diana, the huntress, and Lady Death. Her memory is evoked again in *Campos de Castilla* in the poems devoted to Leonor, Machado's very young wife, so untimely taken away by death. Leonor has disappeared, she has been swallowed up by the land in poems CXX and CXXII (we are reminded of Persephone's abduction by the Lord of the Underworld through a chasm in the earth), and the poet's bitterness is mitigated only by the beautiful thought and the desperate chance that she, like Persephone, might be restored to him in the spring (poems CXV, CXXIV, and CXXVI). It is again the figure of Persephone as the beloved that provides the poetic logic for the traveler's descent into the underworld to rescue his love from the kingdom of death in "Recuerdos de sueño, fiebre y duermivela" ("Memories from Dreaming, Fever and Fitful Sleep"), first published in 1931. The myth of Persephone is distinctly evoked again in "Canciones a Guiomar" (1929), part III, where the poet as lover imagines himself successfully stealing a goddess away from the Lord of the Underworld! And, finally, in "Muerte de Abel Martín" (1933), the identity of the illusive and tantalizing image of woman that haunted the dreams of his earliest poetry is clearly made explicit as Lady Death.

This feminine image with her bipolar significance (springtime and love; destiny and death) is more than just an image of woman. Like the treatment of woman and love in traditional folksong, in the *copla andaluza*, for example, she possesses an allegorical character. She speaks to what is deepest in man's psyche and soul. She is that which is most desirable and most feared; she is the source and the cause of love, pain, pleasure, tragedy, and death. Her poetic treatment is surely related to what Machado is later to call "the metaphysical folklore of our land" (p. 462).[5]

If *Soledades* is the cornerstone of much of Machado's entire literary

9

production, it is no less important to the development of twentieth-century Spanish lyric poetry. It grows out of a rich confluence of late nineteenth-century poetry: the Spanish romanticism of Gustavo Adolfo Bécquer, the French symbolism of Paul Verlaine, and the Latin American modernism of Rubén Darío. But Machado in *Soledades* goes beyond the aesthetics of his great predecessors. The historical importance of his early masterpiece is that it is the first work of Spanish poetry to create a symbolic system according to the principles of composition characteristic of the symbolic systems of modern European poetry. Within this tradition, the poetic work is conceived as a unified totality in which the individual poem loses its relative autonomy (an autonomy still to be found in the poems of Bécquer, Verlaine, and Darío) and becomes vitally dependent on a greater whole of which it forms an organic part. An outgrowth of a great tradition of modern symbolic poetry, reaching back through Baudelaire to William Blake, *Soledades* offers us the first twentieth-century Spanish poetry of self-contemplation, of a crisis of identity, which has required for its enactment the development and elaboration of a complex symbolic system. We will develop this point in detail soon, but, as we have tried to suggest, through the example of the recurrent Persephone figure, a key principle of this new mode of composition leads directly to the great dramas of the mind, embodied in the subsequent symbolic systems of Juan Ramón Jiménez, Rafael Alberti, and Federico García Lorca. In this way, Machado, beginning with *Soledades*, contributes to the growth of artistic consciousness within a brilliant tradition of modern European poetry.

With respect to the historical importance of *Soledades*, we would do well, finally, to heed the observations of the poet himself. In an undated fragment, written about twenty years after his earliest poetic compositions, Machado states:

The anecdotal, the documentary in human affairs, is not by itself poetic. Such was exactly my opinion twenty years ago. My composition "Children's Songs," written in 1898, . . . proclaims the right of lyric poetry to tell of pure emotion, erasing completely the human story. The book *Soledades* was the first Spanish book from which the anecdotal was totally banned. I coincided in advance

10

with what was to be the newest aesthetics. But the agreement of my purpose at that time did not go beyond the abolishment of the anecdotal. (p. 713)

This is a significant statement that has either been ignored or poorly understood by most critics of Machado. Let us leave until later discussion of the significance of Machado's reference to "Children's Songs" and concentrate for the moment on the meaning of the "abolishment of the anecdotal" and the "telling of pure emotion." At first glance we can see an affinity between this affirmation and the symbolist-modernist aesthetic, with its emphasis on the suggestion and expression of feeling, emotion, and states of mind.[6] Machado acknowledges such an affinity, but quite clearly, both here and elsewhere (pp. 46 and 47), he also disassociates himself from the aesthetics of Verlaine and Rubén Darío. He tells us that he was determined to follow a different artistic path.

It seems to me that the key to a better understanding of this "pure emotion" may be found in the pervasive influence of family and teachers on the young Machado. A great uncle, Agustín Durán,[7] a grandmother, Cipriana Álvarez de Machado,[8] and particularly the father, Antonio Machado y Álvarez, were all responsible for the young poet's interest in the folklore, folksongs, and traditional verse of his country. It is important to observe that the essence of Spanish lyrical folksongs, the *copla andaluza*, for example, and within this genre especially, the *cante jondo*, is precisely "to tell of pure emotion."[9] I would suggest, then, that Machado's early aesthetics has its roots deep in his Andalusian heritage. When we recall that the title of one of the poems of *Soledades* is "Cante Hondo" (the learned form of *cante jondo*), we suddenly realize that throughout the entire work there are constant references to "sorrow," "pain," and "anguish," expressed often through the modality of song. Machado's traveler and poetic voice is engaged, to be sure, in a lyrical mode of "deep song." Whether it be to the dramatic guitar of poem XIV ("Cante Hondo") or to the "guitar of the inn" of poem LXXXIII, one aspect of the poetic personality (the traveler) is always sensitive to the "magical music" of his land. Indeed, his attraction to the guitar even prompts him on one occasion (poem LXXVII) to refer to himself as a "moonstruck guitarist." For these rea-

11

sons, I find myself in agreement with J. M. Aguirre who argues that
the title *Soledades* is the learned version of the Andalusian *soleares*,[10]
and that this "deep song" is its inspiration.[11] In this light, the *can-
ciones*, the children's games, the *consejos* (pieces of poetic advice in-
spired in folk sayings), and the *coplas mundanas* (worldly songs) dis-
tributed throughout *Soledades* acquire a special significance.[12] It
seems to me again that Aguirre is correct when he concludes a section
of his study entitled "Simbolismo y Folklore" in this way: "Antonio
Machado has done no more, perhaps, than follow the advice implicit
in the words of his father."[13] And the father's words, cited by Aguirre,
are these: "Learned poets, in my opinion, would not waste their time
by studying them (popular songs) as potential sources of more com-
plex poems."[14]

The significance of this important facet of Machado's early aesthet-
ics is, then, both historical and, to a degree, political. The aesthetics
of *Soledades* is influenced by the progressive liberal ideology of Macha-
do's father, whose respect for the Spanish *pueblo* (common people)[15]
and its folklore is his most valuable legacy to his son. Nowhere is this
legacy better articulated than at the end of the prologue to the father's
early and important collection of flamenco songs, *Cantes flamencos*.
The father concludes modestly but eloquently by justifying his collec-
tion as a necessary bringing together of materials on which a true
science of folklore can be based: "our only purpose has been to gather
materials for that new science destined to vindicate the right of the
pueblo, until now unrecognized, to be considered as an important
factor in the culture and civilization of humanity."[16]

In the final section of this introduction, we will return to a fuller
exploration of the poet's Andalusian heritage and of what it means to
his first poetic masterpiece.

Soledades As a Symbolic System: Main Themes and Expressive Patterns[17]

Let us review briefly what is surely a dominant note in the special
orchestration of this complex work. The ninety-six poems of *Sole-
dades* are both introduced and concluded with an explicit reference to
the loss of youth (in poems I and XCV). And during the course of these

ninety-six poems, there are at least three other explicit references to the loss of youth (in poems XVIII, L, and LXXXV), and numerous expressions of the same theme in less discursive form.[18] The sadness and grief at the loss of youth (or the loss of something in youth) and the search and the yearning to regain what was lost[19] is clearly a unifying element throughout the work.

Furthermore, there is ample evidence to suggest an intricate interrelatedness among all of the poems based on the recurrence of a key vocabulary ("lost youth," "sorrow," "old anguish," "secret," "dream"); the recurrence of key imagery such as the traveler, the road, and the figure of the beloved; and the recurrence of the characteristic landscapes of the soul (garden, park, fountain, roses, orchard, light, etc.). Indeed, there is surprising evidence of coherence of a more formal nature if we examine briefly the beginning and ending of each of the five main sections of *Soledades*. We have already observed how poems I and XVIII of the first division make explicit the theme of lost youth.[20] In "Del Camino," we note a similar reference to prayer and devotion in the first and last poems of this division. In "Canciones," the image of the window is repeated in the first and last poems of this grouping. In "Humorismos, Fantasías, Apuntes," the image of the noria (waterwheel), the title of the opening poem, reappears in the last poem.[21] Finally, in "Galerías" (taken together with the concluding five poems of "Varia"), the "galleries of memory" figure in both the first poem and in the next to last poem of this final major division. Thus, a certain vocabulary or recurring image—a faint echo of some kind—opens and closes, almost imperceptibly, each division of *Soledades*.

Cognizant, then, of this evidence of a special logic that gives each section its identity, we may begin with the eighteen poems of the second subdivision, "Del Camino," and observe how a dominant pattern emerges and how it presides over and is supported by all the other parts of the total composition. From the very first poem, "Prelude," we become conscious of a sense of prayer and religious yearning pervading this section. This is where the figure of the traveler and the road is firmly established and in terms ("pilgrim") that clearly indicate a spiritual quest. We note a key recurring vocabulary ("psalm," "dream," "secret"), and we also note that the object of the traveler's spiritual quest seems to be related to love ("the shadow . . . of a

13

sacred love") and to a special territory ("one pure morning / your boat moored to the other bank," "the green and sacred and flowered land / of your dreams," "mountains yet untrod," "the garden," "your roses," "your lilies"). Nevertheless, the roads and the landscapes over which the traveler conducts his search are just the opposite of the desired territory. What he desires is a springtime atmosphere, an atmosphere of purity and light with gardens and flowers in bloom. What he encounters is a world in decay, presided over by temporality and sterility. The lack of fertility is perhaps the most notable characteristic of the road to be traveled:

upon the bitter land   (XXII)
on the naked earth   (XXIII)
my poor sad shadow / upon the high plain and under a fiery sun
    (XXXVII)

It is as if this land had been smitten by a blight, as attested in poem XXXIII:

My love? . . . Tell me, do you remember
those tender reeds,
languid and yellow,
that stand in the dry riverbed?
    Do you remember the poppy
the summer burned,
the withered poppy,
black crepe of the fields?
    Do you recall the sun, cold
and humble, in the morning,
that glistens and trembles
broken on a frozen fountain?

From the very beginning a strange and supernatural atmosphere seems to envelop these poems. There are rivers to cross, subterranean passages to negotiate, mountains in the distance, special signs from the sky, as well as gardens, fountains, and peaceful landscapes of repose. There is an undercurrent of anxiety and fear in the mind of the traveler. He is searching for something, for someone, that is both desired and feared. On five different occasions, a special hour, a designated time, is mentioned; there is an appointment to be kept:

"My hour!" I cried   (XXI)
the hour in bloom is born   (XXIII)
the hour of an illusion draws near   (XXV)
the rendezvous of a bitter love   (XXX)
But She'll not miss the rendezvous   (XXXV)

This appointment is alternately feared and desired. On two occasions, the encounter to be is with death; on the other three, with an invisible loved one. There is clearly something wrong or felt to be wrong with this lover's tryst. The spiritual presences over infertile land of poem XXV are enveloped at the outset by the plaintive tolling of church bells. The "bitter love" of poem XXX is subtly reinforced by the ambivalent character of the "elusive virgin ever by my side" of poem XXIX.

Thus the pilgrim conducts his quest for fertile ground and fulfillment against the background of a landscape that seems so often to deny the conditions of life he seeks. These are landscapes of the soul, objectifications of what is deeply felt within, which offer a contrast between a potential reality so ardently desired and a present reality so empty and impoverished. These landscapes are also eloquent expressions of inner turmoil and frustration, as we see in the final poem, XXXVII. Here in the intimacy of night, the protagonist pours out his grief and bitterness of heart. He repeatedly asks the personified spirit of the night to explain to him what is wrong. What is the mystery of his secret? What is the nature of his long-standing grief? And the night, like the personified forces [22] of whom the traveler asks questions on so many other occasions, is unable to satisfy him. Nonetheless, poem XXXVII provides an expressive recapitulation of the drama contained in the preceding seventeen poems.

In "Del Camino," then, we encounter the most important and certainly the most tightly knit section of *Soledades*. It is here that the main outline of the spiritual quest takes definite shape. This emerging pattern must be recognized if the other parts of the work are to be fully understood. Now let us consider further aspects of the pilgrim's quest

15

for special territory and, in particular, for his familiar garden land-scapes. The garden (and its equivalents, orchard, park) is not only a central image of the pilgrimage in "Del Camino," it is an image cen-tral to the quest throughout the entire work and recurs with significant frequency. From some of the very first poems (VI and VII), where the garden, the park, the fountain, the fruit trees, and remembered time occupy a position of primary importance, through the "Galerías" (see especially poem LXX, "a garden of eternal spring"), the recurring im-age of the garden gradually acquires a fixed symbolic significance. This "enchanted garden of yesterday" (poem XVIII) is not only the recollected scene of the pilgrim's earliest childhood, it also becomes identified with man's first residence on earth. With its accumulated Edenic associations (of which the fountain is the most important), Machado's garden becomes a symbol of paradise lost, a symbol of lost youth and innocence. The garden, then, is the sacred territory and the goal of the pilgrim's quest, a quest that becomes increasingly a search for lost origins, a homeward journey.[23] This is surely what Dámaso Alonso meant when he wrote a number of years ago with reference to the significance of the orchard: "it is illusion—the blessed golden illusion—seen in the joy and memory of childhood, at the virginal dawn of life and projected also toward the future. It is the paradisical homeland and also the eternal home: the place whence one comes and whither one goes. It is what one dreams and what one lives for."[24] To dream of what was once possessed, to recover what was once lost, to return to an original state of paradise—this is the pattern of experience that begins to emerge in "Del Camino."

We have seen that the pilgrim seems to have an appointment with a loved one, with someone he both desires and fears, as he travels over the desolate landscape of "Del Camino." Yet Machado's expression of the soul's quest for love is by no means rectilinear. The pattern of development follows a kind of recall, common in musical structure, by which a theme, presented in a prelude, but then left behind, emerges within another theme in its progressing development. The presentation of the beloved in Soledades follows just such a pattern. The key poems (X, XVI, and XXXIX), which help define her identity, all lie outside of "Del Camino." But once we have succeeded, with their help, in establishing the special character of the desired woman, it will become apparent how essential this knowledge is to a full appreciation of "Del Camino." In poem X, the beloved is identified with the coming of spring and, as we have seen before, is both feared (or to be avoided) and desired:

. . . .

and, across from me, the house,
and on the house, the iron grating
before the windowpane that slightly blurs
her placid and smiling little face.
I'll stand aside. I don't want
to knock at your window . . . Spring
is coming—her white robe
floats in the air of the dead plaza—;
she is coming to kindle the red
roses of your rosebushes . . . I want to see her.

In poem XVI, the mystery of the elusive virgin deepens. No longer associated with the freshness and purity of springtime, she is pale, bitter, shrouded in black. Special mystery attaches itself to the bridal bed she may be seeking and to the fact that her inhospitable bed may already have been half-violated by an unknown intruder:

Fleeing always and always
near me, the disdainful expression
on your pallid face partly
covered by your black cloak.
I do not know whither you go
nor where your virgin beauty
seeks in the night a bridal bed. I do not know
what dreams your eyelids close,
nor who has half-opened
your inhospitable bed.

. . . .

Pause a moment, elusive
beauty, pause a moment.

17

I should like to kiss the bitter,
bitter flower of your lips.

The definitive clue to the mysterious identity of the beloved is con-
tained in the last stanza of poem XXXIX:

And [woe] to our first love
and its ill-requited faith,
and also to the true
lover of our beloved!

It seems to me that the classical fertility myth of Persephone provides
the answer to our riddle. Persephone, maiden of spring, daughter of
Demeter, was carried off against her will, through a chasm in the
earth, by the Lord of the Underworld. Her mother searched for her
many days in vain, and in her anger and grief, "she cursed the land
. . . making fields lie sterile, blighting seed and crop." [25] Eventually,
Persephone was restored to her mother by the intervention of Zeus.
But because she had eaten in Hades the seeds of a pomegranate, she
was obliged to return to the Underworld and pass there the third part
of every year: "She did indeed rise from the dead every spring, but
she brought with her the memory of where she had come from; with all
her bright beauty there was something strange and awesome about
her." [26] This is the maiden and the myth that inspires Machado's crea-
tion of the "elusive virgin ever by my side." She appears with the
spring, but she brings with her the memory of death. She is at once
the object of the traveler's love and the cause of his bitterness, for she
has another "lover" for part of the year—she is the wife of the Lord of
the Underworld.

If one allows oneself to absorb some of the details of this ancient
myth, one experiences at the level of allegory renewed insight and
pleasure on rereading especially "Del Camino" and "Canciones." We
now understand better the grief and bitterness of the traveler and his
desire for and fear of the appointed hour ("the rendezvous of a bitter
love"). This is the once beautiful world that has been invaded and
violated by the Lord of the Underworld, a "fallen" world punished by
decay and temporality. Machado's pilgrim searches for his loved one

18

as the grieving Demeter searches for her daughter, though the bitterness of the pilgrim is not that of the mother but that of the anguished lover. The figure of Persephone is perhaps Machado's most profound poetic conception. She is the embodiment of two powerful elements in man's deepest emotional composition. As the maiden of springtime, she represents eternal youth and beauty; as the Queen of the Underworld, she presides over the unknown and fearful kingdom of death. She is the destiny of every man, the maiden who beguiles the youthful traveler in the springtime of his years, and the mistress who awaits the final and ultimate consummation at the end of the road of life ("But She will not miss the rendezvous"). Which aspect of her bipolar nature will prevail in the pilgrim's quest? Will this phantom image lead him back to paradise (to a psychological rebirth and renewal), or will it lure him on to the kingdom of death (to an inner domain of sterility and emptiness)? The figure of Persephone, then, embodies all that is most desirable and all that is most fearful; hence the marvelous ambiguity of the poetic image, "elusive virgin ever by my side."

It is important to point out here that this bipolar character of Persephone corresponds to a key pattern of significance perceptible throughout the early poetry. We observe throughout *Soledades* two fields of expressive imagery that contrast the new versus the old, spring versus autumn, fertility versus sterility, morning versus afternoon, dawn versus nightfall, hope versus despair, with a predominance almost always of the negative over the positive. Or to try to express this idea in something of the metaphorical language of the poetry itself, we can say that the traveler (or the speaker) characteristically sings a plaintive song along the roads of an old and harsh and infertile land, trapped in the dust and decay of an unhappy present reality. But he is ever searching for the green fields of the promised land and listening for the happy song of a new sunrise, the pure dawn of a new day. He is attentive, at least for a while, to the possibility of a better future until a somber mood of pessimism and bitter regret at life's lost and stolen opportunities finally prevails. Persephone belongs to all that is fresh and innocent in the promised land of a lost past that may be recovered in the future, and the Queen of the Underworld captures all that is sterile and dead in the stagnant reality of the present.

19

Everywhere in *Soledades,* the emotional and imaginative current of Machado's pilgrim reveals a regular rise and fall as the sense and promise of the quest is felt to be possible, or doubtful, or hopeless ("the maddening postures we assume"). A constant attitude of inquiry is also to be observed as the protagonist looks for answers to unanswerable questions and seeks reassurance from invisible companions all along the way. Early in the work, there are clear indications that an inner division of the poetic personality is interfering with the search for the beloved. Heart and soul, feeling and seeing seem to be in opposition:

In the atmosphere of the afternoon
there floats that aroma of absence
which says to the luminous soul: never,
and to the heart: await.   (poem VII)

Beloved, the breeze tells
of your pure white robe . . .
My eyes will not see you;
my heart awaits you!   (poem XII)

Further insight into the psychic condition of the poetic personality is obtained when we note the presence of an attitude and a spirit quite different from the solemnity and the reverence of the first poem, "Prelude," which initiates the quest of "Del Camino." Beginning with the very first poem of *Soledades,* we note a vein of irony, mockery, and irreverence, almost imperceptible at first, but later unmistakable— an undercurrent of feeling that is disruptive, that detracts from the seriousness and sense of purpose of the pilgrim, and that is responsible for the interruption of a sustained spiritual progression. The pilgrim never seems to be getting anywhere; he appears and reappears in the same set of familiar scenes and situations. Almost as if in response to the mysterious voice that mocks his effort, he returns again and again to relive the same questions and the same experiences, hoping to find a way out of his dilemma. There is no progression; there is no sustained quest, and this is due, I think, to undercurrents of feeling and emotion that are essentially at cross-purposes.

20

The forward movement of one is denied by the restraining movement of the other in a perfect rhythm of frustration.

More insight into the nature of this emotional instability is provided by the important observation of S. Serrano Poncela: "I consider that what is essential in the poetry of 'Soledades' and 'Galerías' is characteristically oneiric."[27] This observation is born out by the dramatic evidence of "Del Camino." As we have seen, this is where the pattern of the spiritual quest acquires shape and form. We note that there are six poems (XXII, XXVII, XXVIII, XXX, XXXIV, and XXXVII) in which reference is made to dreams and to the dreamlike nature of the images of the journey, or to "dream" or "dreams" as something longed for and hoped for—dream as the goal at the end of the quest. In five other poems, reference is made to the illusory and unreal nature of what is dreamed of ("rosy chimeras," "illusion," "white shadows," etc.— XXII, XXV, XXVI, XXXI, and XXXVI). If we take into account this dream-like and dream-inspired character of the quest, we are ready to respond properly to the final poem (XXXVII) of the section, which describes and sums up perfectly the essential nature of the preceding seventeen poems:

Oh, tell me, friendly night, old love
who brings me the puppet stage of my dreams
always empty and forlorn, and
with only my ghost inside,
my poor sad shadow
on the high plain and under a fiery sun,
or dreaming bitter dreams
in the voices of all mysteries,
tell me, if you know, old love, tell me
whether the tears I shed are my own.
The night answered me:
To me you never revealed your secret.
I never knew, my love,
whether you were that ghost of your dream,
nor did I ever find out whether his voice was yours,
or the voice of a grotesque buffoon.

. . . .

21

In order to listen to your complaint from your lips,
I sought you out in your dream,
and there I saw you wandering
in a cloudy maze of mirrors.

"My poor sad shadow / on the high plain and under a fiery sun" describes exactly the figure of the traveler and his environment in many of the preceding poems. Yet these images are seen to be called forth by the "puppet stage of my dreams." It seems clear now that we are supposed to recognize and understand that the adventure of the traveler-pilgrim along the roads of life amidst the desolate and deserted landscapes is a projection of dream and memory images. The quest in *Soledades* is primarily a drama of the mind and a projection of the mind. The special symbolism of the dream images and the mirror images tells us that this is above all the poetry of self-contemplation. The poet looks deep within himself and sees there, reflected on the mirrors of his inner dream world, images of himself and aspects of self from the present and the past. This is the significance of his mournful dialogue with the "friendly night" (really a dialogue with self). Confronted with multiple images of self, he asks which one is his true identity, to which projection of self do the tears really belong? Does the "phantom" who wanders through the labyrinthine world correspond to the dreamer's real identity, or is it a ghost or a voice of his former self—an image or an echo of what once was, but is no longer? This is no ordinary dialogue, then. It is an "intimate monologue" in which the various voices of a split personality break the silence of the solitary wanderer. It is not only a division within one personality, as we have already seen, but a conflict between more than one personality that accounts for the fragmented sensibility of the "hero," reflected throughout *Soledades*. The poet himself reinforces our sense of this crisis of identity in his well-known prologue of 1917: "And I still thought that man can discover a few words of an intimate monologue, distinguishing the living voice from the inert echoes" (p. 47).

The key to a deeper understanding of the poet's "dialogue" with the night lies, I believe, in the expression "the voice of a grotesque buffoon." Indeed, one of the poet's voices (the voice of night) indicates that the ghost of the dream world might speak as the voice of either the traveler or of a grotesque actor, of someone who makes a fool of himself on the stage of the dreamer's imagination.[28] This sense of the grotesque, this awareness of the fool, will guide us now to a more perceptive rereading of "Del Camino." From at least poem XXII on, one notes the recurring presence of a voice offstage, a recurring perception that interrupts the scene to mock, to ridicule, and to despair of the conduct and aspirations of the pilgrim. Sometimes the voice speaks directly and ironically from offstage as in poem XXII ("Little figures that pass by and smile / —an old man's melancholy toys—") or directly and despairingly as in poem XXXV ("Our life now is time and our only concern / is the maddening postures we assume"). At other times, the voice disguises itself and indirectly mocks the enterprise as in poem XXVIII ("A bird hidden . . . a mocking whistle"), or projects (in poem XXX) an image of the pilgrim as a ghostly fool ("At the bend of a shadowy street, / a derisive phantom kisses a purple nard"). Gradually we realize that there is a mocking and ironic vein not only in "Del Camino," but throughout *Soledades*. There is a double presence, two faces of the self, projected onto the stage of the dreamer's imagination—protagonist and analyst, participant and observer, one who searches deeply and desperately and one who mocks the effort. It is this double awareness and this self-irony that accounts for the difficult language of many of the most famous of Machado's early poems: the "manly hypocrisy" of poem I, the "enemy mirror" of poem LXI, and the "hypochondria" of poem LXXVII.

We are now ready to address ourselves to a difficult problem that lies at the heart of the identity crisis. We have already seen at the conclusion of "Del Camino" that the more the poet listens to the voices and observes the images of his inner dream world, the more he is confronted with the reality of a "cloudy maze of mirrors." But if the reality of the inner world is seen to dissolve into a multiplicity of ambivalent images, let us also note that the reality of the external world is equally problematical and elusive. As we reflect upon the twilight world of sunsets and shadows in *Soledades*, we cannot help but ask: is the brother really in the same room as the speaker in poem I, or is there only a picture of the brother on the wall ("A solemn portrait on the wall / still catches the light"), actualized and brought to life in the mind of the speaker? Does the beloved, the image of the

23

feminine figure, really appear to the poet behind the window of the balcony, or is the image (in poems X and XV) merely a projection of the dreamer's fantasy? We begin to recognize the symbolic vehicles through which a solipsist contemplates both within and without. Just as the mirror is the vehicle by which the dreamer gains access to self and to aspects of self, so the window is the medium by which the dreamer so often seeks to communicate with the external world, and, in particular, with the desired loved one.[29] He is seldom in the same "room" as the reality he desires; he is so often separated from it by a window:

> Don't you see, in the charm of the flowery bay window,
> the pink oval of a familiar face?
> Her image, behind the glass of ambiguous gleam,
> comes in and out of focus like an old daguerreotype.   (XV)

> She is a youthful form that one day
> comes to our house.
> We say to her: Why do your return
> to the old home? She opens the window,
> and the whole countryside
> in light and aroma comes in.   (XXXVI)

> Of balconies and windows
> the panes of glass light up,
> with dying reflections,
> like whitish bones
> and half-seen skulls.   (LIV)

> Evening falls opposite the big houses
> in the wide dreaming plaza. The balcony windows
> glitter with the dying echoes of the sun. On the balconies
> are forms that look like vague skulls.   (XCIV)[30]

The observer is afraid, frustrated, and haunted by what is on the other side of the window. He looks for his Persephone figure or for the youthful spirit of his springtime, and he finds only a "fallen" world, temporal, in a state of decay, with signs that Lady Death is near. Even in those few instances when the window (or balcony) is opened and contact seems to be established with the promised reality, the sense of felt significance is almost immediately lost and the "friendly" images, the memories of the beloved or of the sacred territory, dissipate right before the observer's eyes (poems XXV, XXXVI, XXXVIII, and XLIII). We note particularly in poem XXXVI how the friendly images ("the whole countryside in light and aroma") yield right away to the accustomed vaporous unreality ("green smoke," "white mist," "another chimera").

Thus, the poetic voice is both unsure of its own identity and uncertain about the nature of the external world. The seriousness of purpose of the pilgrim is constantly undermined by the dilemma of the solipsist.[31] The traveler is inevitably led to see the absurdity of his position. A world of mirrors, dreams, and mirages (puppet figures on the stage of the imagination) is a distorted and grotesque world and does not provide conditions in which the pilgrimage can be realized. Two deep undercurrents of feeling express themselves, as we have seen, in contradictory ways:

> "Fear not . . ."
>
> .   .   .   .
>
> You will yet sleep many hours
> upon the ancient shore . . .   (XXI)
>
> Little figures that pass by and smile
> —an old man's melancholy toys—   (XXII)
>
> "Open the balcony window. The hour
> of an illusion draws near . . ."   (XXV)
>
> Close at hand, O pilgrim, is
> the green and sacred and flowering land
> of your dreams. . . .   (XXVII)
>
> A bird hidden among the branches
> of the lonely park
> utters a mocking whistle . . .   (XXVIII)

Unsure of its own identity, unable to distinguish the true voice from the many echoes, the poetic self is led to adopt an attitude of irony and mockery towards itself. This is the alter ego, the "enemy mirror" (made explicit in poem LXI, as we will see), that constantly mocks the pilgrim's endeavors. This crisis of identity helps explain the peculiar character of the spiritual quest—why certain elements of the quest are picked up and dropped again almost at random, why the modern pilgrim, in short, never really gets anywhere. The spiritual journey is continually interfered with by projections of the contradictory feelings, images, and attitudes of the alter ego, who does not have faith and who cannot even believe in the reality of the external world.

The opposition of a split personality, then, of the pilgrim's longing to believe and the disbelief of the solipsist (radically skeptical about both the inner and outer worlds), accounts precisely for the conflict of personality—the crisis of identity—that we have been observing all along. The voices and attitudes in opposition can be detected from the very first poem in *Soledades*, but they reach alarming proportions in the section entitled, "Humorismos, Fantasías, Apuntes." Here is where the collision of two powerful undercurrents of attitudes and feelings can be observed in their most concentrated form.

"Humorismos, Fantasías, Apuntes" can be interpreted as a sustained attack by the militant solipsist on the dreams of the pilgrim and on the signs and symbols of his quest. Poem XLVI, "The Noria," presents an ironic commentary on the condition of man ("poor old mule!") and the "divine" poet who rules over his destiny. Poem XLVII, "The Gallows," depicts or conveys the horror of the Crucifixion with none of the promise of Redemption. We note the loss of the desired loved one through time and death in poem XLIX, "Elegy for a Madrigal," and in poem LIV, "Bad Dreams." We also note a parody of the following key elements in the quest: the Edenic garden and fountain in poem LI, "Garden"; the rendezvous with the beloved in poem LII, "Fantasy of an April Night"; and the special fruit trees of the Edenic orchard in poem LIII, "To an Orange and a Lemon Tree." A predominant note of boredom and futility, as it expresses the present, disillusioned sense of the child's world, once felt to be the age of paradise ("my golden youth"), can be observed in poem XLVIII, "Flies," and in Poem LV, "Weariness." Finally, there is a category of poems (LVI, LVII, LVIII, and LX) that convey an especially bitter note of negation and blasphemy. In poem LVIII, for example, we observe that the rivers of life flow into the sea of death, in contrast to the search for a return to

26

origins, a return to the youth-restoring springs at the source of the rivers. And in poem LX, the projection of self is watching and listening "on the shores of the great silence," a dramatic contrast to the earlier posture of the pilgrim who could occasionally sense "the promised land" on the other side of the river (poems XXI and XXVII). At the end of "Humorismos," one senses a dark foreboding of silence and nothingness. Indeed, there are only two occasions when the voice of the pilgrim is heard and in both cases the expression of hope and belief is qualified, in poems L, "Perhaps," and LIX, "Last night when I was asleep."

If we keep in mind this view of "Humorismos, Fantasías, Apuntes" (as an eruption of the irreverence and negation of the solipsist), we are better able to understand the meaning of the introduction to the very next section, "Galerías." As a prelude to the longest and most important of the final two sections of *Soledades*, poem LXI provides key insights into a more complete understanding of the identity crisis. Close attention to its imagery, combined with a knowledge of what immediately precedes and what eventually follows, will prepare us now to arrive at a final sense of the significance of the quest within a divided personality:

Introduction

Reading one bright day
my well-loved verses,
I saw in the profound
mirror of my dreams

a divine truth
trembling with fear,
and it's a flower that wants
to cast its aroma on the wind.

The poet's soul
is oriented to mystery.
Only the poet can
contemplate what's distant
within the soul, in misty,
magical sunlight enveloped.

27

In those endless
galleries of memory,
where the poor folks
hung like a trophy

the gala dress,
moth-eaten and old,
there the poet knows
how to watch the eternal
working of the golden
bees of dreams.

We poets, with our souls
attentive to the deep sky,
in the cruel battle
or in the tranquil garden,

new honey create
with sorrows old,
the pure white robe
we patiently make,
and burnish under the sun
our strong armor of iron.

The enemy mirror,
the soul that doesn't dream,
projects our image
with a grotesque profile.

In our breast
we feel a surge of blood
that passes . . . and we smile
and to our work return.

Thus, poem LXI represents a reaffirmation of the poetic imagination
that favors the image of the pilgrim in his search for "a divine truth."
It also reaffirms at the end, more strongly than ever before, the mental
nature of the quest ("we smile, / and to our work return"). Mystery,
truth, and the symbolic territory ("the tranquil garden"), though spiri-
tually distant goals, are located within the soul and can be objects of

contemplation for only the poet. Only the poet, through the language of poetic imagery, can convert the "moth-eaten" experiences of the past into purified present images. Out of painful past experiences ("old sorrows"—those that accompany the disrupted harmony of the child's world), the poetic imagination can develop the image and the vision necessary for personal salvation. Here, significantly introduced in the first poem of "Galerías," we find the very image ("the pure white robe / we patiently make")[32] that corresponds to the pattern that we have been calling the quest for a Persephone figure. In addition to the presence of the symbolic images of the quest ("the tranquil garden," "the pure white robe"), poem LXI also introduces images of war ("in the cruel battle," "we burnish our strong armor of iron"). If we have been attentive to the contradictory images and voices in the preceding poems, we now understand that the "cruel battle" refers to the conflict of a divided personality, the assault of the militant solipsist on the search for truth of the determined pilgrim. Although we have already suggested the significance of the "enemy mirror," we can now understand more fully in its proper context the difficult eighth stanza:

> The enemy mirror,
> the soul that doesn't dream,
> projects our image
> with a grotesque profile.

"The enemy mirror, / the soul that doesn't dream" has manifested itself repeatedly throughout the preceding section. Indeed, it has done nothing but project grotesque images of the self in "Humorismos," where it clearly won its battle with the pilgrim for supremacy of the mind. How appropriate and dramatic it is, then, that the poetic imagination of the first poem of "Galerías" affirms its determination to defend itself in battle, by adopting the familiar attitude (attentive to "a divine truth") and posture ("dreaming") of the pilgrim, in contrast to the "grotesque" image of the self (wide awake, eyes wide-open, watching and listening "on the shores of the great silence"), projected in the final poem of the preceding section!

The determination to dream and to reconstruct the inner world in accordance with the traveler's quest for rebirth and regeneration is

29

maintained, nonetheless, in very few of the following poems. Though the sense and imagery of the quest continue right through to the very end of *Soledades*,[33] the voice of irony, ridicule, and disgust clearly prevails after poem LXX ("toward a garden of eternal spring / will they one day lead you")—from the "romantic notions long dead" and the "old vulgarities" of poem LXXI, to the strong sense of the grotesque in poems LXXII, LXXV, and LXXVI, and to the awareness of "hypochondria" in poem LXXVII. Poem LXXXV especially provides some important clues on the way we must interpret the outcome of the conflict and the final significance of the quest. First of all, we find an echo of Dante in the first line of the last stanza. "Today, midway in life" recalls the first line of Dante's *Inferno*, "Nel mezzo del cammin di nostra vita." Machado's pilgrim is ending his journey on the very note on which Dante's pilgrim began his journey in the *Inferno*. This is the essential difference between the twentieth-century poet and the medieval poet. Machado's quest is a journey of frustration and futility. It ends as it begins; there is no redemption for the modern pilgrim, lost in a dark world, abandoned on the road of life.

The second detail to be noted is that poem LXXXV makes a distinction between "today" and "yesterday." We may recall that throughout "Del Camino" and in many of the early poems of "Galerías," distinctions between the past and the present tend to be blurred in the indeterminate world of dreams. But now, at the end of *Soledades*, this temporal distinction is crucial. It is introduced here, insisted upon again in the very next poem ("yesterday," "today," "today," "yesterday," "today") and reinforced twice significantly in poem XCV ("Yesterday a poet, today a sad, / poor, time-worn philosopher"). What is this crucial difference between today and yesterday? The answer lies in the last two lines of poem LXXX: "O never-lived youthful days, / if only I might dream you again!" The poet can no longer even dream his unlived youth. Poem LXXXV thus announces the loss of the very capacity to dream that was seen to be the essential activity by which the soul protected its spiritual self from the "enemy mirror" in the first poem of "Galerías." Again poem LXXXVI hammers away at this present inability of the mind to work miracles with yesterday's "griefs" and "sorrows." Yesterday's mental fertility is repeatedly compared with

30

today's sterility. Poem LXXXIX offers one final reminder ("on this sad day when you walk / with your eyes wide open") that self-knowledge may still be gained by remembering cloudy projections of past dreaming. But it is ultimately hopeless. The words and the imagery of Ecclesiastes ("all is vanity and a striving after wind")[34] prevail over the pilgrim's desire to dream the road back to rebirth and mother (poem LXXXVII). Dust, wind, smoke, musical dissonance, and the presence of death all testify in the final poems to the sterility of the inner landscapes of the soul.

By the end of "Galerías," then, the projections of self have assumed postures (eyes opened), adopted roles (cynical philosopher in place of dreaming poet), and developed attitudes ("we know nothing at all of our souls") that stand in striking contrast to those enunciated at the beginning of the section. A full circle has been completed. The pessimism and the projections of a "grotesque profile" of "Humorismos" by the "enemy mirror, the soul that doesn't dream" have returned to haunt the poet. The sense of sterility is too strong, the wind of futility is everywhere in evidence, for the spirit of Ecclesiastes triumphs over the hope for redemption of the pilgrim-traveler. All the various images and symbols, through which the poetic self externalizes the bipolar nature of its inner life, come into play with the clear surrender of one personality to another—the devout pilgrim yields to the "bitter sage," the infant to the old man, the spirit of springtime to the specter of death, the dreaming poet to the embittered philosopher, unable to sleep or dream.

Now it is necessary to modify the earlier description of a dominant mode of feeling and emotion occasioned by the loss of youth and the desire to regain lost innocence; for we have discovered in the course of this study the presence of another mode of thought and feeling provoked by a crisis of personality. There are two personalities competing for supremacy over the psychic constitution of the self. The ideals and goals of the traveler are under constant attack by the skepticism of the militant solipsist. It is the genius of Machado to have discovered a symbolic mode of expression adequate to the demands of a consciousness at war with itself. The powerful and contradictory emotions of a divided personality are converted into objects for aesthetic contemplation by the symbolism of the quest and by the symbolism of the language of dreams. *Soledades* thus presents a drama of the mind, a modern psychic projecton of an ancient quest for lost origins, in which the twentieth-century "hero" suffers defeat and participates in parodying that defeat—an achievement that has produced the first masterpiece of twentieth-century Spanish lyric poetry.

Soledades and the "Problem of Spain"

Even after we have achieved some insight into the dilemma of the traveler, there still remains the tantalizing question: What is the root cause of this crisis of personality? What are the deeper reasons for the frustration of this quest for regeneration through youth, love, and happiness? Just what is it that has shattered the dreams of a better life and produced the skepticism that prevails at the end? The general theme of lost youth is clear and comprehensible enough, but surely there is more in *Soledades* than general expressions of regret, nostalgia, and bitterness at the passing of time and lost opportunities. Why the special sense of unlived youth? What accounts for the traveler's bitter sense of a life that has passed him by, the special sense of being cheated and robbed of life's most precious possession?

As we have seen, the traveler of Machado's world is haunted by dreams and visions of unrealized adventure. The closest that he comes to telling us what is wrong with him, is couched explicitly but mysteriously in only one poem, XVIII, entitled "The Poet," which ends on this cryptic note: "O Soul, that tried in vain to be younger each day, / pluck your flower, the humble flower of melancholy!" It seems to me that much of the significance of Machado's early poetry is contained in this one poetic concept, of wanting, but vainly trying to be younger each day. The point would seem to be that the speaker was young once but not young enough. This is what has kept him from love, from happiness, and from realizing his beautiful dreams of springtime. This would seem to be the meaning behind the mysterious refrain "It's a bright afternoon, / almost spring-like" of poem VII, in which the image of remembered youth, under the protective shadow of mother, comes so close to grasping the enchanted fruit in the waters of the fountain. But the fruit is not quite reachable, the season is not quite springtime, because, however paradoxical it may sound, the child is not quite young enough.

Worth remembering at this point is a key principle of literary criticism that Machado articulated in the 1920s: "Every work of art, however humble, will always lie within the ideology and the mode of feeling of an epoch. There exist, to be sure, works that are behind their times and works that are in tune with their times; but they always belong to a spiritual climate that one comes to know" (p. 827). Let us recall, therefore, that Machado was raised in a Republican family and schooled by both liberal teachers and Republican friends. He was prepared to participate in a new and better Spain. He was influenced from the beginning by the patriotic dreams and aspirations for "a young and fertile Spain" of his teacher Francisco Giner. When his traveler-pilgrim of *Soledades* searches for pure fountains, lost gardens, Edenic fruit, maternal images, virgin goddesses, and eternal spring, is this not a metaphorical expression of Giner's own vision of rejuvenated individuals and a regenerated society?

But the traveler of *Soledades* does not encounter the promised land; he does not experience rejuvenation; he feels alienated and discouraged by the images of life and death in the world around him. Furthermore, the traveler is not the only victim of this frustrated aspiration for renewal and regeneration. What chance do children have for a better future when they are trapped in the old streets of dead cities (poem III), like the recurring image of the waters of life and youth, trapped in the old stone fountains? What, indeed, lies ahead for these children when their education is bound by tradition and marked by the shadow of Cain (poem V), and where their agricultural and social systems are still stamped by the waterwheel and the gallows, as in poems XIII, XLVI, and XLVII? Though the drama of *Soledades* is primarily a personal one, the images and problems of a larger social reality also make themselves felt. The dusty roads, the barren fields, the beggars ever present near churches, the desolate and unpopulated landscapes of *Soledades* not only reflect the spiritual state of its traveler, they capture aspects of the reality of Spain, filtered through the dreamlike world of the poetic consciousness. Hence the significance of the recurring word "old." The imagery of "old Spain" is everywhere in evidence, and overwhelms with its presence the delicate and fragile hopes for the dawn of a new day ("one pure morning," "to burn new aromas / on mountains yet untrod," "the joyful music of a pure dawn").

Herein, it seems to me, lies the mystery of the treatment of youth in *Soledades*—the meaning of "unlived youth," the images of premature aging, of growing old without growing up, and the sense of disillusionment and defeat. The difficulty with being young, or, in terms of the poetic language of poem XVIII, the futility of trying to be "younger each day," is the result of being trapped in a decadent and archaic society. As Manuel Tuñón de Lara states: "While the whole world threw itself into the exalting adventure of the twentieth century, Spain was still a prisoner of the life patterns of other times."[35] This is the historical reality that conditions, in the words of Machado, the "spiritual climate" of his epoch.

The dilemma of the traveler of *Soledades* corresponds, then, to the historical and social problems of modern Spain. It belongs to the whole history of defeat and disillusionment suffered by the democratic tradition of Spanish liberalism to which Machado belonged. Indeed, the desire for regeneration and modernization is the frustrated dream of Spanish liberals going back to Mariano José de Larra and even earlier. The best and most eloquent voices of criticism and protest are directed against an oligarchical system and society that excluded them, ignored them or persecuted them, and wasted the abilities and energies of their most talented youth. If there is any doubt about the historical and social significance of Machado's treatment of youth, one has only to recall some of the key texts within this tradition. Larra writes in an article of April 1833, a few months before the death of Ferdinand VII, when hopes for a liberal Spain were still darkened by the survival of Absolutism: "The boys of the enlightened nineteenth century . . . get to be old men without ever having been young."[36]

More than sixty years later, in 1895, Miguel de Unamuno wrote his well-known series of essays entitled "En torno al casticismo." The failure of the revolutionary years of 1868 to 1874, the bankruptcy of the Restoration system, and the resumption of the disastrous colonial wars in Cuba are all on his mind when he makes this famous commentary: "This is the terrible word: there is no youth. There may be young people but youth is missing. And the fact is that latent inquisition and senile formalism repress it. . . . There is no Young Spain nor anything like it, nor any protest beyond the one that seeks a refuge at café tables, where talent is squandered and vigor, illspent."[37] Seven years later, in a less well-known essay, written in December 1902 and entitled "Old Men and Young Men," Unamuno ends his article on this note, which surely has its effect on the youthful author of *Soledades:* "Of course every man born is a new-born man; but the men we need are not merely new ones but even newer, newest, ones who have been renewed."[38]

Finally, Antonio Ramos-Gascón reminds us of the special sense of "young" and "old," as expressed in one of the important journals, *Germinal,* at the turn of the century. The following quote, taken from one of the contributors to *Germinal,* shows clearly, in one precise way, how Machado's poetic vocabulary was influenced by a certain "spiritual climate" of his time:

> Time neither gives nor takes away youth. Dante called it the spring of life and many old men die in full flower without ever having known that sad winter which cools the blood and withers the freshness and vigor of ideas. All those are young who have within their breast a liberal heart; those who understand existence as a fertile sacrifice for the future; those lovers of the ideal that had sufficient power to rejuvenate Faust.
>
> Few years are not youth. Pidal was a fossil within a few hours of his begetting; Larra if he were still living would be as much a lad as when he began to sprout whiskers. That's the way "youth" is understood by those of us who gather round *Germinal.*[39]

Seen now against the background of the democratic liberal tradition of nineteenth-century Spain, the theme of lost and unlived youth acquires its full historical significance. In the tradition of Larra, Giner, and Unamuno, Machado elaborates poetically the same patriotic concern: the problem of being a young person in an old society. How much more fully do we understand now the mysterious and plaintive line of poem XVIII of *Soledades* ("O Soul, that tried in vain to be younger each day")! What chance does the speaker have of being

35

really young ("newer" or "newest" in Unamuno's sense) when he is caught in a society "still a prisoner of the life patterns of other times?" He cannot respond, therefore, to the "something that passes / and never arrives" (poem VIII). This mysterious something is, of course, youth, love, and happiness, because the solitary traveler of Machado's world is possessed, to use the exact words of Giner, "by the presentiment of a new and better life." The terrible dilemma of *Soledades* is that the speaker wants desperately to respond to the images of springtime that he senses in the world around him and to the vital sap of youth that he knows must flow within him. But he is unable to be deeply affected by these vital forces of regeneration. The quest is a failure, the promises of spring remain unfulfilled, his youth is unlived and lost forever. Therefore, at the end of *Soledades*, the mysterious reality that earlier was sensed as something present or close at hand becomes "something that didn't quite arrive, / all that has now gone away" (poem XCIII). The drama of *Soledades* is the frustrated adventure and emotion of a "moonstruck guitarist," who wants to join in the happy song of a new day, but who is everywhere haunted by the unhappy sights and sounds of a world in decay.

The Aesthetic and Ideological Significance of Machado's Andalusian Heritage

It is now possible to return to Machado's important observations on the aesthetics of *Soledades* commented on in the first section of this introduction. There we explored the significance of the poet's words, the "abolition of the anecdotal" and the "telling of pure emotion," leaving aside until now the full implications of this statement on children's songs: "My composition 'Children's Songs,' written in 1898 . . . , proclaims the right of lyric poetry to tell of pure emotion, erasing completely the human story." This reference is to the second poem of the first edition (1903), which appears, with its title and dedication (to Rubén Darío) removed, as the eighth poem of the 1907 and later editions. It is highly significant, I think, that this mysterious phrase, "of something that passes / and never arrives," is sung by children in a poem singled out for special attention by the author. The key stanza of this intriguing poem is the next to the last one:

36

The children were singing
ingenuous songs,
of something that passes
and never arrives:
the story confused
and the sorrow clear.

Here, indeed, in the songs of young children, is the "pure emotion"
and "erased history" of which Machado speaks.

It is time now to see the correspondence between the emotion of
these children's songs and that of the song of the traveler himself, in
his musical dialogue with the fountain of poem VI. He returns to the
fountain to ask questions about his past, questions that have to do
with love and unsatisfied yearnings. We note again the theme of pure
emotion and vague, forgotten history ("the story confused / and the
sorrow clear") in the same disquieting atmosphere of laughter and
sadness:

"I don't know what your laughing song
tells me of faraway dreams, sister fountain.

I know that your clear crystal of joy
once tasted the flame-colored fruit of the tree;
I know that faraway is that bitterness of mine
which dreams of the old summer afternoon.

I know that your fair singing mirrors
copied raptures of love affairs long gone:
but tell me, fountain of enchanted tongue,
tell me my forgotten legend of joy."

"I know no legends of long-gone joy,
only melancholy stories of old.

It was on a bright afternoon of the slow summer . . .
You came alone with your sorrow, brother;
your lips kissed my pure waters serene,
and in the bright afternoon their sorrow they told.

Your burning lips told their sorrow;
the thirst they now feel, they also felt then."

37

"Goodbye forever, sonorous fountain,
eternal singer of the sleeping garden.
Goodbye forever, your monotonous tune,
O fountain, is more bitter than my sorrow."

Alan Trueblood has seen something essential when he observes that poem VIII "reveals how well Machado's ear is attuned from the start, no doubt in consequence of his father's active interest in folklore, to the communal voice in poetry and song."[40] Thus, the traveler in search of lost and unlived youth is attuning his voice from the very beginning to the communal voice of the common people, here embodied in the songs and games of children. The actual fusion of the individual voice with the communal is well exemplified by the popular *copla* in poem XI.[41] In it we may recognize again the poetic treatment of "pure emotion" and "erased history." The "Deep Song" of just three poems later continues to reveal, in the most dramatic terms, just how Machado's traveler is affected by the "magical music" of his land. Indeed, two of the essential themes of his *Soledades*, love and death, are here evoked in personified and allegorical form:[42]

. . . And it was Love, like a red flame . . .
—A sinewy hand on the vibrating string
struck a long golden sigh
that changed into a fountain of stars—.

. . . And it was Death, a grim skeleton,
the blade on her shoulder, her step long.
—As she was when I dreamed of her as a child—.

And on the guitar, resonant and tremulous,
the sudden hand, as it struck, simulated
a coffin coming to rest on the ground.

And a lonely lament was the gust of wind
that sweeps the dust and the ashes away.

The "Love" of "Deep Song" is conceived as both a "red flame" of passion and a precious nostalgia for a fountain of stars ("a long golden sigh / that changed into a fountain of stars"). How subtly this imagery of love is further developed by that of poem XL, "Gallant Inventory,"

38

again of traditional verse and popular inspiration. Love as passion or as ideality expresses itself in this poem as the dèsire for a dark gypsy woman under "black moonless nights / beside the salty sea," or as a desire to render homage (to make a white bouquet) for the fair and pretty sister who "is a morning star in the distant blue." How is the traveler to reconcile the fiery passions of love, which quickly turn to ashes, with the ideal of love, which, like a star, is so inaccessible and inhuman?

The proximity of sadness and happiness, the inevitable conversion of joy into pain, is the theme of the very next poem (XLI) and, in fact, is closely related to the bipolar significance of the Persephone figure that haunts the traveler on the roads of life. His is a spiritual quest for an ideal maiden of springtime, constantly threatened and spoiled by the proximity of Lady Death. For this reason, the traveler's rendezvous with love is so often menaced and interrupted by this fearful and ill-fated intruder:

> The whole evening glows
> with a nightmarish light.
> The sun stands in the West.
> The echo of my step resounds.
>
> "Is it you? I was waiting for you . . ."
>
> "You're not the one I was looking for."
>
> (LIV, "Bad Dreams")

Enough evidence has been presented, I think to suggest how Machado's interest in folklore and in folksongs has greatly enriched his resources as a cultivated poet. His *canciones, consejos,* and *co-plas*—his cultivation of traditional meter and popular inspiration[43]— comment poetically on the quest, generalize the experience of the traveler, and insert it within a traditional Andalusian vision of the world. His attunement of the individual voice to the communal voice of his people is one more way by which he has achieved the intricate linking and interaction of the ninety-six poems that constitute the symbolic system of *Soledades.*

Having studied earlier the contemporary tradition and spiritual climate that condition the "pure emotion" of Machado's solitary traveler, we have still to inquire into the "emotion" ("the erased history and the clear sorrow") of which the children sing. If the poetic voice of *Soledades* does attune itself to the communal voices of its land, it behooves us now to inquire into the meaning of these voices. This is, of course, the most difficult of all the questions we have posed, and we cannot do more than offer a provisional answer in the form of a hypothesis. In volumes II and III of the *Biblioteca de las tradiciones populares españolas*,[44] there are major sections devoted to collections of children's games in Extremadura. In the prologue, the author of these volumes pays his respects to the poet's father, A. Machado y Álvarez, for the idea that children's songs and games carry within them "the spirit of other generations, reminiscences of times that were,"[45] an accredited idea among the folklorists of the time, which recurs several times in the commentary that accompanies the songs in the collection. Indeed, the father himself in the "Postscript" of his *Cantes flamencos* repeats the idea in this way:

> Children unconsciously conserve in their games the memory of the past, and, by putting their memory and their powerful instinct for imitation at the service of these apparent trivialities, perpetuate the testimony of truly primitive monuments in human history, by means of which the historian and early man enrich their knowledge. The poetry of childhood . . . is, by this concept, very interesting.[46]

This unconscious remembrance of things past, this collective memory of what once was, is directly related to the observation of Joaquín Costa, who says in his book *Poesía popular* that "our whole history projects its shadow over our folk poetry."[47]

Therefore, our task is to recall, however briefly, the nature of this national history that casts its shadow over the popular lyrical folksongs. What is the relationship between this history and the memories and traces it leaves in the songs of Machado's land and particularly in the *copla andaluza*?[48] What does "deep song" tell us about what Dámaso Alonso has earlier described (in note 42) as the "mysteries and central problems of man"? Rafael Cansinos-Assens, in a brilliant series of essays, entitled *La copla andaluza*, suggests an answer in terms that are very appropriate to the early poetry of Antonio Machado. Cansinos-Assens's essays are infused with a fine sensitivity

40

to the historical injustices of Spanish national life. He argues convincingly that in the depths of the *copla andaluza* there lies not only an intimate drama, but a collective drama. The *copla* has its roots deep in the collective historical experience of persecuted minorities: Arab, Jew, and Gypsy, for whom censorship, exile, and death are a recurring pattern throughout Spain's national history. Cansinos-Assens is careful to point out that the *copla* is not characteristically political or even historical in nature. It is typically the powerful expression of emotion—love, pain, fatal and tragic sense of life—of the individual singer. But it is an emotion that grows out of, to use the language of Machado, the "erased history" of a persecuted and oppressed humanity. Let us listen to the rhetorical questions of Cansinos-Assens, so attuned to Machado's own sense of an emotion, particularly an emotion of love, whose origin and cause are confused or have been forgotten.

> In this *copla* of love, so passionate and sensual, to which we listen, will we perceive, without knowing it, the funeral song of those oppressed races who have lost the precise memory of the cause of their tears, but not the sense of their mourning and their habit of lamentation? What racial nostalgias, what secular affront, what arcane sorrows do they discreetly lament under the allegory of these erotic *coplas* lending them their solemn religious accents? What drama of a whole people is expressed in this affliction of love, what drama of a whole people was only saved by the guitar from the disaster in which it lost the psalter and the psalm, the altar and the gods?[49]

Cansinos-Assens goes on to propose a speculative answer to these questions.

> . . . It is not possible to forget the historical drama: the terrors those passionate men have seen, the horrors that those descendants of converted Jews have survived, the silent melancholy, in which they were begotten by fathers to whom not even complaint was allowed. Everything conspires to suggest an oriental origin for those songs. The Judeo-Moorish hypothesis, the Gypsy hypothesis. Either of the two carries with it a precious and frightful load of lost

41

treasures, of disasters, in which only love was saved, and even this, battered and grieving, participating in the general havoc. Because love, in the *copla*, is not a star of good luck; on the contrary, it is overtaken by universal disillusionment and is subject, like everything else, to the risks of fate.[50]

Cansinos-Assens's exquisite sensitivity deepens our appreciation of the emotional and spiritual climate of Machado's *Soledades:* the unlived treasures of youth, the promises of life that never quite arrive, the sense of exile, the nostalgia for a lost golden age, the allegorical treatment of love, the shadow of pain or fear that hovers over happiness, the fright at the unknown intruder, the mysteries of destiny, the mystical almost religious character of the *copla* (which recalls the traveler's "psalms" in the quest of "Del Camino"), the sorrow and the suffering, the bitterness and the blasphemy. Though it is particularly the Andalusian heritage operating here, we must also note Machado's sensitivity to images and symbols (the beggar, the waterwheel, and the gallows) that capture the harsh conditions of life in Old Spain (certainly Castile as well as Andalusia) and show him to be responsive at an early age to the life of the humble and wretched peoples of his land. His own alienation, his own state of spiritual exile, lead him to identify his condition with that of other marginalized and dispossessed peoples, especially in backward rural Spain.

Thus, Machado captures in his *Soledades* not only something of the "spiritual climate" of his time (the bitterness and despair, and the desire for something better, occasioned by the disasters of national life at the turn of the century), he also attunes his poetic voice to the folksongs of his Andalusian heritage and evokes the deep song of sorrow and sadness as well as the striving for happiness that characterizes the collective historical drama of a downtrodden but resilient humanity.

I have meant to suggest several parallels between the personal drama of Machado's traveler and the collective drama of Andalusian people. There are, of course, inevitable differences arising from the social situation and mentality of a middle-class poet. The luxury of self-contemplation, of daydreaming, and of boredom will be criticized by the poet himself as he moves on to a more committed and combative position with respect to the social ills of his society. Nevertheless, even in the earliest poetry of *Soledades*, we can appreciate the first efforts of an educated middle-class poet to approach and draw upon artistic forms of knowing and feeling of his Andalusian people. To return once again to one of Machado's key statements about his early aesthetics ("My composition 'Children's Songs' . . . proclaims the right of lyric poetry to tell of pure emotion"), we can finally recognize, I think, that Machado is looking past the undeniable influences of Rubén Darío and Paul Verlaine and pointing to the folksong and pure emotion of his Andalusian culture as a primary source of aesthetic inspiration. In so doing, Machado carries forward and brings into greater prominence a tendency perceptible in lyric poets throughout nineteenth-century Spanish literature. As José Pedro Díaz observes of Spanish poets, particularly of the 1850s and 60s:

> . . . The apprenticeship they served working on German literature and a few examples of French literature led our writers to pay attention to the poetic voice of the humble people. But the folk voice they listened to was that of their own *pueblo*, and especially that which is heard in *cantares* and *soleares*, those that do not create fictional characters, nor narrate, but express directly the emotion of the singer.[51]

Of all of Machado's most immediate literary forebears, the most important is, without a doubt, his great Sevillian predecessor, G. A. Bécquer,[52] whose best and deepest lyricism was also nourished by the *copla*, the *soleá*, and the *cantar*.[53] But unlike Bécquer, who felt more comfortable with the values of the past, Machado was a progressive liberal, educated to believe in the value, equality, and future potential of his *pueblo*. He brings to his cultivation of popular poetry, therefore, a statement of principle couched in republican and democratic language ("proclaims the right of lyric poetry to tell of pure emotion"). In the aesthetics of his *Soledades*, Machado, as poet, echoes his father, as folklorist in the spirit of scientific inquiry, in defending "the right of the *pueblo*, up to now unrecognized, to be considered an important factor in the culture and civilization of humanity."

Michael P. Predmore
Stanford, California

43

Notes

1 *Spain (1808–1939)* (Oxford: At the Clarendon Press, 1966), p. 469.

2 Machado's three volumes of poetry may be translated as follows: *Solitudes, Galleries and Other Poems, Lands of Castile,* and *New Songs.* Of these three translated titles only the last one is reasonably accurate. Other translators have tried other versions but none fully succeed because words like *Soledades* (related to a long tradition of popular poetry) have meanings and associations that cannot be captured economically, if at all, by their supposed equivalents in English. For convenience and simplicity, I will refer to these volumes in Spanish as *Soledades, Campos de Castilla,* and *Nuevas canciones.* For this same reason, I will also refer to the various subdivisions of *Soledades* by their Spanish titles. Translations of all Spanish titles and subtitles are included in the Table of Contents. For Machado's collected works, I use the Spanish title, *Poesías completas,* which contains, in addition to his poetry, a few essays in prose. All references in this study to Machado's poetry and prose (page numbers in parentheses in Introduction) will be to the edition of Aurora de Albornoz and Guillermo de Torre, *Obras: Poesía y prosa* (Buenos Aires: Losada, 1964).

3 *Antonio Machado: Selected Poems* (Cambridge: Harvard University Press, 1982), pp. 14–15.

4 *Estudios sobre Unamuno y Machado* (Madrid: Guadarrama, 1959), pp. 295–96.

5 Machado's younger colleague, Federico García Lorca, also expresses the "metaphysical folklore" of Andalusia in terms so appropriate to Machado's treatment of his "elusive virgin ever by my side." With reference to specific *coplas* of the *cante jondo,* Lorca says: ". . . the verses have a common background: Love and Death . . . , but a love and a death seen through the Sibyl, that personage who is so oriental, true sphinx of Andalusia," "El cante jondo," *Obras completas* (Valencia: Aguilar, 1965), pp. 45–46.

6 See Ed Baker, "Machado recuerda a Pablo Iglesias," *Ideologies and Literature* 1, no. 3 (May-June 1977), particularly pp. 13 and 14.

7 The collector and compiler of the *Romancero general* (1849–51), one of the most important collections of ballads of the time.

8 See Paulo de Carvalho-Neto, *La influencia del folklore en Antonio Machado* (Madrid: Ed. Demófilo, 1975) for a brief account of this remarkable woman's collaboration in the folkloric studies of her son and of her influence on her grandchildren, pp. 107–8.

9 "The *cante grande (jondo)* is the original expression of flamenco. It is the pure *cante,* the trunk from which all other *cantes* branch. In its oldest form it was derived from ancient religious chants and songs, which later developed into a more generalized lament of life. This category, consisting basically of *cantes* originally gypsy-inspired, includes by far the most difficult group of *cantes* to interpret," D. E. Pohren, *The Art of Flamenco* (Morón de la Frontera: Society of Spanish Studies, Finca Espartero, 1972), p. 48. For an eloquent description of this song's capacity to convey "the most infinite gradations of Sorrow and Pain, placed at the service of the most pure and exact expression," see the above article of García Lorca, "El cante jondo," pp. 45–49.

44

10 "The *soleares* have been described as the 'mother of the *Cante*.' This, of course, is a poetic allusion, more likely referring to the role that the *soleares* play in flamenco—there is no doubt that they are the central figure, the matriarch, around which all of flamenco revolves—than to any belief that the *soleares* have given birth to flamenco," Pohren, *The Art of Flamenco*, p. 145. For an authoritative discussion of the etymology and origins of the *soleares*, see the fundamental book of Ricardo Molina and Antonio Mairena, *Mundo y formas del cante flamenco* (Madrid: Revista de Occidente, 1963).

11 Aguirre, *Antonio Machado, poeta simbolista* (Madrid: Taurus, 1982), p. 71.

12 For a detailed description of the influence of popular verse forms and traditional meters on Machado, even in his earliest "modernist" phase, see the account of Tomás Navarro Tomás, "La versificación de Antonio Machado," *Antonio Machado: El Escritor y la Crítica*, ed. by Ricardo Gullón and Allen W. Phillips (Madrid: Taurus, 1973), pp. 273–89.

13 *Antonio Machado, poeta simbolista*, p. 72. Aguirre does well to call our attention to a special facet of French symbolism: "its admiration for folklore in general and its acceptance of popular poetry in particular," p. 63.

14 *Antonio Machado, poeta simbolista*, p. 61. For the complete context of this statement, see the prologue to *Cantes flamencos* (Madrid: Espasa-Calpe, 1975), ed. Antonio Machado y Alvarez, p. 19.

15 *Pueblo* in Spanish has no simple translation in English. For our purposes it is sufficient to call attention to the humble peoples, particularly those of the countryside, whose age-old suffering is so poignantly reflected in their folksongs. We will retain, therefore, the Spanish word throughout this introduction.

16 *Cantes flamencos* (Madrid: Ed. Cultura Hispánica, 1975), p. 49. Notice that this is a different collection and edition than that cited in note 14.

17 Much of this section of the introduction is a modified version of my article, "The Nostalgia for Paradise and the Dilemma of Solipsism in the Early Poetry of Antonio Machado," *Revista Hispánica Moderna*, núms. 1–2 (1974–75), 30–52.

18 The clearest examples are provided by the following poems: III, VI, VII, VIII, IX, XXXVI, XLI, LXII, LXVIII, LXXIV, LXXVII, LXXVIII, and XCIII.

19 In an early article, R. L. Predmore was one of the first to point to an affinity between Machado and Proust with respect to the search for lost time. See "El Tiempo en la Poesía de Antonio Machado," *Publication of the Modern Language Association* 63 (June 1948): 708–9.

20 The last poem (XIX) of this subdivision, like poem XCVI (in relation to XCV), offers an expressive variation on the dominant theme. Here in XIX, we note the psychic and spiritual difference between the young girl and the older man. She, in the innocence of youth (totally unself-conscious), is not affected by the sight and presence of the man. She, like the children of poem XCVI, still belongs to the paradise of youth and innocence, while the little old man (of poem XCVI) and the speaker (of this poem) represent the state of man "after the fall," after the loss of innocence.

21 For insightful commentary on the "waterwheel" poems, see Ramón de Zubiría, *La poesía de Antonio Machado* (Madrid: Gredos, 1966), pp. 156–57.

22 Which are really personifications of an aspect of self. See again Zubiría, pp. 28–

31. There are many important aspects of this poem that will be commented upon later. But, for the moment, we can note the similarity here between the poet's dialogue with the night and his dialogue with the fountain in poem VI. In both poems, the speaker is interested in discovering a secret about himself; in both poems, "sorrow," "pain," and "bitterness" describe the inner condition. In both poems, the answers to the speaker's questions are not supplied.

23 We notice throughout *Soledades* that the traveler responds nostalgically to or yearns for the most intimate and most emotionally charged elements of his earliest childhood: mother, hearth, and native land. See poems VII, XIV, XXV, LIII, LIX, LXVII, LXXX, LXXXIII, and LXXXVII.

24 "Poesías olvidadas de Antonio Machado," *Poetas españoles contemporáneos* (Madrid: Gredos, 1965), p. 135.

25 Ovid, *Metamorphoses*, trans. Rolfe Humphries (Bloomington: Indiana University Press, 1968), p. 122.

26 Edith Hamilton, *Mythology* (Boston: Little, Brown, 1959), p. 54.

27 "Borrosos laberintos," *La Torre*, núms. 45–46 (1964), p. 268. This is an essential article and is to be highly recommended. See as well the insightful article by Willis Barnstone, "Sueño y paisaje en la poesía de Antonio Machado," *La Torre*, núms. 45–46 (1964), 127–39.

28 I am indebted to Paul Ilie for his discussion of the images of the grotesque actor. I believe that Ilie has made the first serious attempt to deal with the poetry of self-contemplation and with the dilemma of personality in the early Machado. See his "Antonio Machado and the Grotesque," *Journal of Aesthetics and Art Criticism* 22 (Winter 1963), especially pp. 214–15.

29 In this regard, Concha Zardoya has commented well on the function of "cristal." See "El cristal y el espejo en la poesía de Antonio Machado," *Poesía española contemporánea* (Madrid: Guadarrama, 1961), p. 189.

30 For further examples, which include the related symbol of "balcón," see poems I, X, XIV, XXV, XXX, XXXVIII, XLV, LII, LVI, LXXII, and XCI.

31 This problem of perception and of belief develops into a major theme ("the existence and the non-existence of the other") in the later prose of Juan de Mairena, well treated by Sánchez-Barbudo in his *Estudios*. See particularly pp. 252–53.

32 We recall the association of "white robe" with "spring" in poem X and with the "beloved" in poem XII, and we see its identification with the "loving hand" of poem LXIV, which we can later identify as mother in poem LXXXVII.

33 In the last poem, "Winter Sun," for example, we observe a whole series of images that, in the ironic mode to which we have become accustomed, signal defeat of the pilgrim's quest: the park (related to the garden of lost youth) frozen in winter, the perfect specter of death and the Underworld; the fruit trees of the Edenic garden profaned by man's pitiful and thoroughly artificial attempts to extend the life of his "lost paradise"; the fountain of running water, sacred in another age for its purifying and youth-restoring powers, now an expressive image of a potential force ("glides," "runs") converted into a perfect image of sterility, as it futilely licks "the greenish stone." We sense also the tremendous distance between the old man (the defeated traveler) in his solitude and the children (so briefly referred to, as brief as youth itself), playing collectively nearby.

34 With the clue provided by the poet in poem XVIII ("with the bitter sage he said: Vanity of vanities"—the "bitter sage" is replaced by "Eclesiastés" in the first edition of *Poesías completas*), I believe we can identify the "sage" of poem LXXXVII and the imagery of the wind in these final poems (LXXVIII, LXXIX, LXXXI, XC, and XCI) as an allusion to Ecclesiastes and to his sense of life and the world.

35 *La España del siglo XIX*, vol. 2 (Barcelona: Ed. Laia, 1976), p. 144.

36 "Don Cándido Buenfé o el camino de la gloria," *En este país y otros artículos* (Madrid: Alianza, 1969), p. 98.

37 "En torno al casticismo" (part 5, section 3), *Ensayos*, vol. 1 (Madrid: Aguilar, 1964), pp. 128, 130.

38 *Ensayos*, vol. 1, p. 438.

39 Antonio Ramos-Gascón, "La revista 'Germinal' y los planteamientos estéticos de la 'gente nueva,'" *La crisis de fin de siglo: Ideología y literatura* (Barcelona: Ariel, 1975), p. 129.

40 *Antonio Machado: Selected Poems*, p. 24.

41 Again well observed by Trueblood: "In the *copla*, the interpolated song, Machado is stylizing a traditional folk-motif in keeping with a long-standing tradition which, in Spain, continues to favor interaction between cultivated and popular art strains," ibid., p. 23.

42 Dámaso Alonso is the first critic, and for many years the only critic, to call our attention to the significance of this poem and its evocation of the Andalusian *copla:* "Antonio has sought, tried, legitimately, to go beyond the momentary to what endures; in a unique accord he has associated his aptitude for living, the music of his land and the desolate landscape." The critic also observes that the reader finds in this poem "not only the evocation of the Andalusian *copla*, but also its intimate meaning, its profound link to the soul of Spain and to its landscape and to its indestructible union with the mysteries and central problems of man," "Ligereza y gravedad en la poesía de Manuel Machado," *Poetas españoles contemporáneos* (Madrid: Gredos, 1965), pp. 92–93. Most recently Manuel Urbano has again called our attention to the importance of this poem. See his "Antonio Machado y el cante jondo: Notas para una propuesta de lectura andaluza," *Cuadernos Hispanoamericanos* 373 (julio 1981), p. 98.

43 See again Navarro Tomás in note 12.

44 The poet's father, Antonio Machado y Alvarez, was the director of one of the earliest projects of collecting materials of Spanish folklore. This collection, which consists of eleven volumes, was published in Seville in 1884 and is entitled *Biblioteca de las tradiciones populares españolas*.

45 *Biblioteca de las tradiciones populares españolas*, vol. 2 (Sevilla: Alejandro Guichot y Compañía, Editores, 1884), p. 107.

46 *Cantes flamencos* (Ed. Cultura Hispánica), p. 315.

47 Cited by Machado y Álvarez in his *Cantes flamencos* (Ed. Cultura Hispánica), p. 294. Joaquín Costa was an eminent jurist, historian, and scholar of the time and friend of the Machado family.

48 I have been using the term *copla* in a broad and generic sense to refer to lyrical folksongs of a traditional character or inspiration. *Copla* may refer, therefore, to *canción, cantar, canto,* and *cante.* For specialists in the field, there are, of

course, subtle distinctions. One can turn immediately, for example, to the father, Antonio Machado y Álvarez, in his *Cantes flamencos* (Ed. Cultura Hispánica), where he points to subtle and fine differences between *cantares* and *coplas*, pp. 304–13.

49 *La copla andaluza* (Madrid: Ediciones Demófilo, 1976), p. 22.

50 *La copla andaluza*, p. 30. Here are two further examples of Cansinos-Assens's eloquence on this subject: "In the Andalusian *copla* there sobs as in a vast Miserere all the irredeemable sorrow of a people, all the irredeemable sorrow of humanity, although expressed in the accents of personal and intimate mourning. . . . The Andalusian *copla* expresses the inevitable passion of those men and women who sing it, . . . exasperated by the injustices of history," pp. 29–30. For further confirmation of this hypothesis, see the moving and well documented account of Félix Grande, *Memoria del flamenco*, 2 vols. (Madrid: Espasa-Calpe, 1979).

51 *Gustavo Adolfo Bécquer: Vida y poesía* (Madrid: Gredos, 1964), p. 272.

52 Juan Ramón Jiménez expresses a special preference for the Antonio Machado who is "the delicate disciple of Bécquer; son of French symbolism, so Spanish, so Andalusian . . . the best Antonio Machado . . .," "Historias de España y Méjico," *Relaciones entre Antonio Machado y Juan Ramón Jiménez* (Pisa: Università di Pisa, 1964), ed. and comp. Ricardo Gullón, p. 86.

53 José Pedro Díaz, p. 251.

SOLEDADES ✳ SOLITUDES

I
(El viajero)

Está en la sala familiar, sombría,
y entre nosotros, el querido hermano
que en el sueño infantil de un claro día
vimos partir hacia un país lejano.

Hoy tiene ya las sienes plateadas,
un gris mechón sobre la angosta frente;
y la fría inquietud de sus miradas
revela un alma casi toda ausente.

Deshójanse las copas otoñales
del parque mustio y viejo.
La tarde, tras los húmedos cristales,
se pinta, y en el fondo del espejo.

El rostro del hermano se ilumina
suavemente. ¿Floridos desengaños
dorados por la tarde que declina?
¿Ansias de vida nueva en nuevos años?

¿Lamentará la juventud perdida?
Lejos quedó—la pobre loba—muerta.
¿La blanca juventud nunca vivida
teme, que ha de cantar ante su puerta?

¿Sonríe al sol de oro
de la tierra de un sueño no encontrada;
y ve su nave hender el mar sonoro,
de viento y luz la blanca vela hinchada?

Él ha visto las hojas otoñales,
amarillas, rodar, las olorosas
ramas del eucalipto, los rosales
que enseñan otra vez sus blancas rosas.

Y este dolor que añora o desconfía
el temblor de una lágrima reprime,

I

(The Traveler)

In the somber family living room
and in our midst, is the beloved brother
who one bright day in a childhood dream
we saw depart toward a distant land.

Today his temples are already silvered,
a gray lock of hair on his narrow brow;
the cold disquiet of his glance
reveals a soul almost totally absent.

The tree tops of the faded old park
are losing their autumn leaves.
The afternoon is painted behind the damp
window panes and in the depths of the mirror.

Our brother's face is lighted
softly. Disillusions in flower
bathed in gold by the waning afternoon?
Yearnings for new life in new years?

Does he lament his lost youth, we wonder?
Far away it died—poor she-wolf?
Does he fear his never-lived white
youth, because it will howl at his door?

Is he smiling at the golden sun
of a dreamland never found;
and does he see his ship cleave the sounding sea,
its white sail swollen with wind and light?

He has seen the yellow autumn
leaves swirling about, the fragrant
eucalyptus branches, the rose bushes
showing again their white roses.

And this yearning or mistrusting sorrow
holds back the trembling of a tear,

y un resto de viril hipocresía
en el semblante pálido se imprime.

Serio retrato en la pared clarea
todavía. Nosotros divagamos.
En la tristeza del hogar golpea
el tic-tac del reloj. Todos callamos.

and a trace of manly hypocrisy
is imprest upon his pallid face.

    A solemn portrait on the wall
still catches the light. We ramble on.
In the sadness of our hearth there beats
the tick-tock of the clock. We all fall silent.

II

He andado muchos caminos,
he abierto muchas veredas;
he navegado en cien mares
y atracado en cien riberas.

En todas partes he visto
caravanas de tristeza,
soberbios y melancólicos
borrachos de sombra negra,

y pedantones al paño
que miran, callan, y piensan
que saben, porque no beben
el vino de las tabernas.

Mala gente que camina
y va apestando la tierra . . .

Y en todas partes he visto
gentes que danzan o juegan,
cuando pueden, y laboran
sus cuatro palmos de tierra.

Nunca, si llegan a un sitio,
preguntan adónde llegan.
Cuando caminan, cabalgan
a lomos de mula vieja,

y no conocen la prisa
ni aun en los días de fiesta.
Donde hay vino, beben vino;
donde no hay vino, agua fresca.

Son buenas gentes que viven,
laboran, pasan y sueñan,
y en un día como tantos,
descansan bajo la tierra.

II

I have walked many roads,
I have opened many paths;
I have sailed a hundred seas,
and moored to a hundred shores.

Everywhere I have seen
caravans of sadness,
proud and melancholy men,
drunk with black shadow,

and offstage pedants
who watch, say nothing and think
they know, because they don't
drink the tavern wine.

Evil people who walk about
corrupting the land . . .

And everywhere I have seen
those who dance or play,
when they can, and till
their small parcels of land.

Never, if they come to a place,
do they ask where they have come.
When they travel, they ride
on the back of an old mule,

and they do not know haste,
not even on feast days.
Where there is wine, they drink wine;
where there is no wine, cool water.

They are good people who live,
labor, pass by and dream,
and on a day, like so many others,
they rest beneath the ground.

III

La plaza y los naranjos encendidos
con sus frutas redondas y risueñas.

Tumulto de pequeños colegiales
que, el salir en desorden de la escuela,
llenan al aire de la plaza en sombra
con la algazara de sus voces nuevas.

¡Alegría infantil en los rincones
de las ciudades muertas! . . .
¡Y algo nuestro de ayer, que todavía
vemos vagar por estas calles viejas!

III

The plaza and the orange trees alight
with their round and smiling fruit.

Tumult of little school children
who, rushing pell-mell out of class,
fill the air of the shaded plaza
with the din of their new voices.

Childhood joy in the corners
of dead cities! . . .
And something of our yesterdays that still
we see wander through these old streets!

IV
(En el entierro de un amigo)

Tierra le dieron una tarde horrible
del mes de julio, bajo el sol de fuego.

A un paso de la abierta sepultura,
había rosas de podridos pétalos,
entre geranios de áspera fragancia
y roja flor. El cielo
puro y azul. Corría
un aire fuerte y seco.

De los gruesos cordeles suspendido,
pesadamente, descender hicieron
el ataúd al fondo de la fosa
los dos sepultureros . . .

Y al reposar sonó un recio golpe,
solemne, en el silencio.

Un golpe de ataúd en tierra es algo
perfectamente serio.

Sobre la negra caja se rompían
los pesados terrones polvorientos . . .

El aire se llevaba
de la honda fosa el blanquecino aliento.

—Y tú, sin sombra ya, duerme y reposa,
larga paz a tus huesos . . .

Definitivamente,
duerme un sueño tranquilo y verdadero.

IV

(At the Burial of a Friend)

They covered him with earth one horrible afternoon
in the month of July, under a fiery sun.

A step from the open grave
were roses with rotten petals,
among geraniums of acrid fragrance
and red blossoms. The sky,
clear and blue. A strong
dry wind was blowing.

Suspended by stout ropes,
the coffin was ponderously lowered
to the bottom of the grave
by the two gravediggers . . .

As it came to rest, a loud, solemn
thump resounded in the silence.

The thump of a coffin against the ground
is something perfectly serious.

Upon the black box the heavy
dusty clods broke up . . .

From the deep grave,
the wind carried off the whitish breath.

"And you, shadowless now, sleep and rest,
long peace to your bones . . ."

Now and forever,
he sleeps a true and tranquil sleep.

V

(Recuerdo infantil)

Una tarde parda y fría
de invierno. Los colegiales
estudian. Monotonía
de lluvia tras los cristales.

Es la clase. En un cartel
se representa a Caín
fugitivo, y muerto Abel,
junto a una mancha carmín.

Con timbre sonoro y hueco
truena el maestro, un anciano
mal vestido, enjuto y seco,
que lleva un libro en la mano.

Y todo un coro infantil
va cantando la lección:
mil veces ciento, cien mil,
mil veces mil, un millón.

Una tarde parda y fría
de invierno. Los colegiales
estudian. Monotonía
de la lluvia en los cristales.

V
(Childhood Memory)

A gray, cold afternoon
in winter. The school children
are studying. Monotony
of rain beyond the window panes.

It is the class. On a poster
Cain is shown a fugitive,
and Abel dead,
beside a crimson stain.

With loud and pompous timbre
the teacher thunders, an old man
badly dressed, lean and dry,
holding a book in his hand.

And a whole children's chorus
is chanting the lesson:
a thousand hundreds, one hundred thousand;
a thousand thousands, one million.

A gray, cold afternoon
in winter. The school children
are studying. Monotony
of the rain on the window panes.

VI

Fue una clara tarde, triste y soñolienta
tarde de verano. La hiedra asomaba
al muro del parque, negra y polvorienta . . .
        La fuente sonaba.

Rechinó en la vieja cancela mi llave;
con agrio ruido abrióse la puerta
de hierro mohoso y, al cerrarse, grave
golpeó el silencio de la tarde muerta.

En el solitario parque, la sonora
copla borbollante del agua cantora
me guió a la fuente. La fuente vertía
sobre el blanco mármol su monotonía.

La fuente cantaba: ¿Te recuerda, hermano,
un sueño lejano mi canto presente?
Fue una tarde lenta del lento verano.

Respondí a la fuente:
No recuerdo, hermana,
mas sé que tu copla presente es lejana.

Fue esta misma tarde: mi cristal vertía
como hoy sobre el mármol su monotonía.
¿Recuerdas, hermano? . . . Los mirtos talares,
que ves, sombreaban los claros cantares
que escuchas. Del rubio color de la llama,
el fruto maduro pendía de la rama,
lo mismo que ahora. ¿Recuerdas, hermano? . . .
Fue esta misma lenta tarde de verano.

—No sé qué me dice tu copla riente
de ensueños lejanos, hermana la fuente.

Yo sé que tu claro cristal de alegría
ya supo del árbol la fruta bermeja;
yo sé que es lejana la amargura mía
que sueña en la tarde de verano vieja.

VI

It was a bright afternoon, a sad and drowsy
summer afternoon. The ivy, black and dusty,
could be seen on the wall of the garden . . .
       The fountain was sounding.

My key grated as it turned in the lock;
with a harsh noise the rusty old gate
came open and, on swinging to, struck
the silence of the dead afternoon a heavy blow.

In the solitary garden, the sonorous
burbling verse of the singing water
guided me to the fountain. The fountain
played on the white marble its monotonous tune.

The fountain was singing: "Brother, does
my present song remind you of a distant dream?
It was a slow afternoon in the slow summer time."

I replied to the fountain:
"I do not remember, sister,
but I know that your present song comes from afar."

"It was this same afternoon: my crystal
played on marble its monotonous tune, just as today.
Do you remember, brother? . . . The well-trimmed myrtles
you see gave their shade to the clear songs
you hear. The ripe fruit, the golden color
of flame, hung from the branch,
just as today. Do you remember, brother? . . .
It was on this same slow summer afternoon."

"I don't know what your laughing song
tells me of faraway dreams, sister fountain.

I know that your clear crystal of joy
once tasted the flame-colored fruit of the tree;
I know that faraway is that bitterness of mine
which dreams of the old summer afternoon.

Yo sé que tus bellos espejos cantores
copiaron antiguos delirios de amores:
mas cuéntame, fuente de lengua encantada,
cuéntame mi alegre leyenda olvidada.

—Yo no sé leyendas de antigua alegría,
sino historias viejas de melancolía.

Fue una clara tarde del lento verano . . .
Tú venías solo con tu pena, hermano;
tus labios besaron mi linfa serena,
y en la clara tarde, dijeron tu pena.

Dijeron tu pena tus labios que ardían;
la sed que ahora tienen, entonces tenían.

—Adiós para siempre, la fuente sonora,
del parque dormido eterna cantora.
Adiós para siempre, tu monotonía,
fuente, es más amarga que la pena mía.

Rechinó en la vieja cancela mi llave;
con agrio ruido abrióse la puerta
de hierro mohoso y, al cerrarse, grave
sonó en el silencio de la tarde muerta.

I know that your fair singing mirrors
copied raptures of love affairs long gone:
but tell me, fountain of enchanted tongue,
tell me my forgotten legend of joy."

"I know no legends of long-gone joy,
only melancholy stories of old.

It was on a bright afternoon of the slow summer . . .
You came alone with your sorrow, brother;
your lips kissed my pure waters serene,
and in the bright afternoon their sorrow they told.

Your burning lips told their sorrow;
the thirst they now feel, they also felt then."

"Goodbye forever, sonorous fountain,
eternal singer of the sleeping garden.
Goodbye forever, your monotonous tune,
O fountain, is more bitter than my sorrow."

My key grated as it turned in the lock;
with a harsh noise the rusty old gate
came open and, on swinging to,
sounded heavy in the silent dead afternoon.

VII

El limonero lánguido suspende
una pálida rama polvorienta,
sobre el encanto de la fuente limpia,
y allá en el fondo sueñan
los frutos de oro . . .

                    Es una tarde clara,
casi de primavera,
tibia tarde de marzo,
que el hálito de abril cercano lleva;
y estoy solo, en el patio silencioso,
buscando una ilusión cándida y vieja:
alguna sombra sobre el blanco muro,
algún recuerdo, en el pretil de piedra
de la fuente dormido, o, en el aire,
algún vagar de túnica ligera.

En el ambiente de la tarde flota
ese aroma de ausencia,
que dice al alma luminosa: nunca,
y al corazón: espera.

Ese aroma que evoca los fantasmas
de las fragancias vírgenes y muertas.

Sí, te recuerdo, tarde alegre y clara,
casi de primavera,
tarde sin flores, cuando me traías
el buen perfume de la hierbabuena,
y de la buena albahaca,
que tenía mi madre en sus macetas.

Que tú me viste hundir mis manos puras
en el agua serena,
para alcanzar los frutos encantados
que hoy en el fondo de la fuente sueñan . . .

Sí, te conozco, tarde alegre y clara,
casi de primavera.

VII

The languid lemon tree droops
a dusty pale branch
over the magic spell of the clear fountain,
and there at its bottom
the golden fruits are dreaming . . .

                It's a bright afternoon,
almost springlike,
a mild afternoon in March,
which carries a breath of April near;
and I am alone in the silent patio,
seeking a simple illusion from the past:
some shadow on the white wall,
some memory asleep on the stone rim
of the fountain, or, in the air,
some light tunic wandering by.

In the atmosphere of the afternoon
there floats that aroma of absence
which says to the luminous soul: never,
and to the heart: await.

That aroma evoking the phantoms
of fragrances virgin and dead.

Yes, I remember you, cheerful and bright afternoon,
almost springlike,
afternoon without blossoms, when you
brought me the good perfume of mint
and of the good sweet basil
my mother kept in her flowerpots.

For you saw me plunge my innocent hands
into the serene water
to reach the enchanted fruits
that today at the bottom of the fountain dream . . .

Yes, I know you, cheerful and bright afternoon,
almost springlike.

67

VIII

Yo escucho los cantos
de viejas cadencias,
que los niños cantan
cuando en coro* juegan,
y vierten en coro
sus almas que sueñan,
cual vierten sus aguas
las fuentes de piedra:
con monotonías
de risas eternas,
que no son alegres,
con lágrimas viejas,
que no son amargas
y dicen tristezas,
tristezas de amores
de antiguas leyendas.

En los labios niños,
las canciones llevan
confusa la historia
y clara la pena;
como clara el agua
lleva su conseja
de viejos amores,
que nunca se cuentan.

Jugando, a la sombra
de una plaza vieja,
los niños cantaban . . .

La fuente de piedra
vertía su eterno
cristal de leyenda.

Corro (circle) might make more sense than *coro* (chorus), but most editions, including the *Obras completas* of 1936, say *coro*.

VIII

I listen to the songs
of cadences old,
sung by the children
when in chorus they play
and pour out in chorus
their dreaming souls,
as the fountains of stone
their waters pour forth:
with monotonous sounds
of eternal laughs,
that are not happy,
with old tears
that are not bitter
and tell sad stories,
sad stories of love affairs
from legends of old.

On the children's lips,
the songs carry
the story confused
and the sorrow clear;
as clear as the water
carries its tale
of old love affairs
that never are told.

Playing in the shade
of a plaza old,
the children were singing . . .

The fountain of stone
poured forth its eternal
crystal of legend.

Cantaban los niños
canciones ingenuas,
de un algo que pasa
y que nunca llega:
la historia confusa
y clara la pena.

Seguía su cuento
la fuente serena;
borrada la historia,
contaba la pena.

The children were singing
ingenuous songs,
of something that passes
and never arrives:
the story confused
and the sorrow clear.

The serene fountain
went on with its story:
with the story erased,
of the sorrow it told.

IX

(Orillas del Duero)

Se ha asomado una cigüeña a lo alto del campanario.
Girando en torno a la torre y al caserón solitario,
ya las golondrinas chillan. Pasaron del blanco invierno,
de nevascas y ventiscas los crudos soplos de infierno.

Es una tibia mañana.
El sol calienta un poquito la pobre tierra soriana.

Pasados los verdes pinos,
casi azules, primavera
se ve brotar en los finos
chopos de la carretera
y del río. El Duero corre, terso y mudo, mansamente.
El campo parece, más que joven, adolescente.

Entre las hierbas alguna humilde flor ha nacido,
azul o blanca. ¡Belleza del campo apenas florido,
y mística primavera!

¡Chopos del camino blanco, álamos de la ribera,
espuma de la montaña
ante la azul lejanía,
sol del día, claro día!
¡Hermosa tierra de España!

IX
(On the Banks of the River Duero)

A stork has appeared on top of the belfry.
Wheeling about the tower and the solitary mansion,
the swallows already pipe their shrill notes. Gone are the
infernal raw winds of white winter with its snowfalls and blizzards.

It is a mild morning.
The sun warms a bit the poor Sorian land.

Beyond the green, almost
blue, pines, spring
can be seen putting forth its new buds
on the slender black poplars along the highway
and the river. Smooth and silent, the Duero flows gently by.
The countryside seems more adolescent than young.

Among the grasses, a few humble flowers, blue or white,
have come up. Beauty of the countryside barely in bloom
and mystical spring!

Black poplars along the white road, poplars on the river bank,
foam of the mountain
against the distant blue,
sun, sun of the bright day!
O fair land of Spain!

73

X

A la desierta plaza
conduce un laberinto de callejas.
A un lado, el viejo paredón sombrío
de una ruinosa iglesia;
a otro lado, la tapia blanquecina
de un huerto de cipreses y palmeras,
y, frente a mí, la casa,
y en la casa, la reja,
ante el cristal que levemente empaña
su figurilla plácida y risueña.
Me apartaré. No quiero
llamar a tu ventana . . . Primavera
viene—su veste blanca
flota en el aire de la plaza muerta—;
viene a encender las rosas
rojas de tus rosales . . . Quiero verla . . .

X

    To the deserted plaza
a labyrinth of alleys lead.
On one side the somber old wall
of a ruinous church;
on the other side, the whitish adobe wall
of an orchard of cypress and palms,
and, across from me, the house,
and on the house, the iron grating
before the windowpane that slightly blurs
her placid and smiling little face.
I'll stand aside. I don't want
to knock at your window . . . Spring
is coming—her white robe
floats in the air of the dead plaza—;
she is coming to kindle the red
roses of your rosebushes . . . I want to see her.

XI

Yo voy soñando caminos
de la tarde. ¡Las colinas
doradas, los verdes pinos,
las polvorientas encinas! . . .
¿Adónde el camino irá?
Yo voy cantando, viajero
a lo largo del sendero . . .
—La tarde cayendo está—.
"En el corazón tenía
la espina de una pasión;
logré arrancármela un día:
ya no siento el corazón."

Y todo el campo un momento
se queda, mudo y sombrío,
meditando. Suena el viento
en los álamos del río.

La tarde más se oscurece;
y el camino que serpea
y débilmente blanquea,
se enturbia y desaparece.

Mi cantar vuelve a plañir:
"Aguda espina dorada,
quién te pudiera sentir
en el corazón clavada."

XI

I move in dreams along
afternoon roads. Golden hills,
green pines,
dusty encinas!*
Where can the road lead?
I am singing along
my traveler's path . . .
The afternoon is waning.
"My heart was pierced
by the thorn of a passion;
I managed one day to pull it out:
I feel my heart no longer."

And for a moment the whole countryside,
silent and somber, remains pensive.
The wind sounds
in the poplars by the river.

The afternoon turns darker;
and the winding road,
now faintly white,
grows dim and disappears.

Again my song laments:
"Sharp golden thorn,
if only I might feel you
into my heart thrust deep."

---

*The encina is the ilex or holm oak, a modest-sized, drab, evergreen oak very common in central Spain.

XII

Amada, el aura dice
tu pura veste blanca . . .
No te verán mis ojos;
¡mi corazón te aguarda!

El viento me ha traído
tu nombre en la mañana;
el eco de tus pasos
repite la montaña . . .
No te verán mis ojos;
¡mi corazón te aguarda!

En las sombrías torres
repican las campanas . . .
No te verán mis ojos;
¡mi corazón te aguarda!

Los golpes del martillo
dicen la negra caja;
y el sitio de la fosa,
los golpes de la azada . . .
No te verán mis ojos;
¡mi corazón te aguarda!

XII

Beloved, the breeze tells
of your pure white robe . . .
My eyes will not see you;
my heart awaits you!

The wind has brought me
your name in the morning;
the mountain repeats
the echo of your steps . . .
My eyes will not see you;
my heart awaits you!

In the somber towers
the bells ring out . . .
My eyes will not see you;
my heart awaits you!

The hammer blows tell
of the black box;
and the strokes of the spade,
the site of the grave . . .
My eyes will not see you;
my heart awaits you!

XIII

Hacia un ocaso radiante
caminaba el sol de estío,
y era, entre nubes de fuego, una trompeta gigante,
tras de los álamos verdes de las márgenes del río.

Dentro de un olmo sonaba la sempiterna tijera
de la cigarra cantora, el monorritmo jovial,
entre metal y madera,
que es la canción estival.

En una huerta sombría,
giraban los cangilones de la noria soñolienta.
Bajo las ramas oscuras el son del agua se oía.
Era una tarde de julio, luminosa y polvorienta.

Yo iba haciendo mi camino,
absorto en el solitario crepúsculo campesino.

Y pensaba: "¡Hermosa tarde, nota de la lira inmensa
toda desdén y armonía;
hermosa tarde, tú curas la pobre melancolía
de este rincón vanidoso, oscuro rincón que piensa!"

Pasaba el agua rizada bajo los ojos del puente.
Lejos la ciudad dormía,
como cubierta de un mago fanal de oro trasparente.
Bajo los arcos de piedra el agua clara corría.

Los últimos arreboles coronaban las colinas
manchadas de olivos grises y de negruzcas encinas.
Yo caminaba cansado,
sintiendo la vieja angustia que hace el corazón pesado.

XIII

Toward a radiant sunset
the summer sun was traveling,
and it was, among clouds of fire, a gigantic trumpet
behind the green poplars on the bank of the river.

In an elm was heard the everlasting scissors
of the singing cicada, the jovial monorhythm,
between metal and wood,
that is the song of summer.

In a shady garden
the buckets of the drowsy noria* revolved.
Under the dark branches the sound of the water was heard.
It was a July afternoon, luminous and dusty.

I was making my way along,
absorbed in the lonely country twilight.

And I was thinking: "Beautiful afternoon, note
of the immense lyre, all disdain and harmony;
beautiful afternoon, you cure the poor melancholy
of this vain niche, dark thinking niche!"

The purling water passed under the spans of the bridge.
In the distance the city slept,
as though covered by a magic half globe of transparent gold.
Under the stone arches the clear water ran.

The last red clouds crowned the hills
dotted with gray olives and blackish encinas.
I was walking along tired,
feeling that old anguish that makes the heart heavy.

---

*I have decided not to translate *noria*, since it figures in some English dictionaries
and is important in its own right. A kind of waterwheel introduced into Spain by the
Arabs, it runs by mule power. Until midcentury it was a common sight in rural Spain.
The endless circling of the well by the mule has much to suggest about the state of
Spanish culture when Machado was writing. See poems XLVI, LX, LXXXVI.

El agua en sombra pasaba tan melancólicamente,
bajo los arcos del puente,
como si al pasar dijera:

"Apenas desamarrada
la pobre barca, viajero, del árbol de la ribera,
se canta: no somos nada.
Donde acaba el pobre río la inmensa mar nos espera."

Bajo los ojos del puente pasaba el agua sombría.
(Yo pensaba: ¡el alma mía!)

Y me detuve un momento,
en la tarde, a meditar . . .
¿Qué es esta gota en el viento
que grita al mar: soy el mar?

Vibraba el aire asordado
por los élitros cantores que hacen el campo sonoro,
cual si estuviera sembrado
de campanitas de oro.

En el azul fulguraba
un lucero diamantino.
Cálido viento soplaba
alborotando el camino.

Yo, en la tarde polvorienta,
hacia la ciudad volvía.
Sonaban los cangilones de la noria soñolienta.
Bajo las ramas oscuras caer el agua se oía.

The shaded water passed so melancholically
under the arches of the bridge,
as though in passing it were saying:

"No sooner is our little boat
untied, O traveler, from the tree on the shore,
when the song begins: We are nothing.
Where the poor river ends, the vast sea awaits us."

Under the spans of the bridge the dark water passed.
(I thought: my own soul!)

And I paused a moment
in the afternoon to meditate . . .
What is this droplet in the wind
that shouts to the sea: I am the sea?

The air was vibrant, deafened
by the singing wings that make the countryside sonorous,
as though it were sown
with little golden bells.

In the blue there glowed
a star as bright as a diamond.
A warm wind was blowing
stirring up the dust on the road.

In the dusty afternoon, I
went back toward the city.
The buckets of the drowsy noria were sounding.
Under the dark branches the falling water could be heard.

XIV
(Cante hondo)

Yo meditaba absorto, devanando
los hilos del hastío y la tristeza,
cuando llegó a mi oído,
por la ventana de mi estancia, abierta

a una caliente noche de verano,
el plañir de una copla soñolienta,
quebrada por los trémolos sombríos
de las músicas magas de mi tierra.

. . . Y era el Amor, como una roja llama . . .
—Nerviosa mano en la vibrante cuerda
ponía un largo suspirar de oro,
que se trocaba en surtidor de estrellas—.

. . . Y era la Muerte, al hombro la cuchilla,
el paso largo, torva y esquelética.
—Tal cuando yo era niño la soñaba—.

Y en la guitarra, resonante y trémula,
la brusca mano, al golpear, fingía
el reposar de un ataúd en tierra.

Y era un plañido solitario el soplo
que el polvo barre y la ceniza avienta.

XIV

(Deep Song)

I was meditating absorbed, spinning
the threads of boredom and sadness,
when there reached my ear,
through the window of my room, open

to a hot summer night,
the mournful sound of a somnolent song,
broken by the dark tremolos
of the magical music of my land.

. . . And it was Love, like a red flame . . .
—A sinewy hand on the vibrating string
struck a long golden sigh
that changed into a fountain of stars—.

. . . And it was Death, a grim skeleton,
the blade on her shoulder, her step long.
—As she was when I dreamed of her as a child—.

And on the guitar, resonant and tremulous,
the sudden hand, as it struck, simulated
a coffin coming to rest on the ground.

And a lonely lament was the gust of wind
that sweeps the dust and the ashes away.

XV

La calle en sombra. Ocultan los altos caserones
el sol que muere; hay ecos de luz en los balcones.

¿No ves, en el encanto del mirador florido,
el óvalo rosado de un rostro conocido?

La imagen, tras el vidrio de equívoco reflejo,
surge o se apaga como daguerrotipo viejo.

Suena en la calle sólo el ruido de tu paso;
se extinguen lentamente los ecos del ocaso.

¡Oh, angustia! Pesa y duele el corazón . . . ¿Es ella?
No puede ser . . . Camina . . . En el azul, la estrella.

XVI

Siempre fugitiva y siempre
cerca de mí, en negro manto
mal cubierto el desdeñoso
gesto de tu rostro pálido.
No sé adónde vas, ni dónde
tu virgen belleza tálamo
busca en la noche. No sé
qué sueños cierran tus párpados,
ni de quien haya entreabierto
tu lecho inhospitalario.

. . . .

Detén el paso, belleza
esquiva, detén el paso.

Besar quisiera la amarga,
amarga flor de tus labios.

XV

The street in shadow. The big tall houses hide
the dying sun; there are echos of light on the balconies.

Don't you see, in the charm of the flowery bay window,
the pink oval of a familiar face?

Her image, behind the glass of ambiguous gleam,
comes in and out of focus like an old daguerreotype.

In the street only the noise of your step resounds;
the echoes of sunset fade slowly away.

Oh, anguish! The heart is heavy and sore . . . Is it she?
It cannot be . . . Walk on . . . In the blue, the star.

XVI

Fleeing always and always
near me, the disdainful expression
on your pallid face partly
covered by your black cloak.
I know not whither you go
nor where your virgin beauty
seeks in the night a bridal bed. I do not know
what dreams your eyelids close,
nor who has half-opened
your inhospitable bed.

. . . .

Pause a moment, elusive
beauty, pause a moment.

I should like to kiss the bitter,
bitter flower of your lips.

87

XVII
(Horizonte)

En una tarde clara y amplia como el hastío,
cuando su lanza blande el tórrido verano,
copiaban el fantasma de un grave sueño mío
mil sombras en teoría, enhiestas sobre el llano.

La gloria del ocaso era un purpúreo espejo,
era un cristal de llamas, que al infinito viejo
iba arrojando el grave soñar en la llanura . . .
Y yo sentí la espuela sonora de mi paso
repercutir lejana en el sangriento ocaso,
y más allá, la alegre canción de un alba pura.

XVII
(Horizon)

On a bright afternoon, as wide as weariness,
when torrid summer brandishes its lance,
a thousand imagined shadows, upright on the plain,
were copying the ghost of a dream of mine.

The glory of the sunset was a purple mirror,
it was a flaming lens which to old infinity
projected my solemn dreaming on the plain . . .
And I heard the sonorous spur of my step
reverberate far off against the bloody sunset,
and beyond, the joyful music of a pure dawn.

XVIII

(El poeta)
Para el libro *La casa de la primavera*
de Gregorio Martínez Sierra

Maldiciendo su destino
como Glauco, el dios marino,
mira, turbia la pupila
de llanto, el mar, que le debe su blanca virgen Scyla.

Él sabe que un dios más fuerte
con la sustancia inmortal está jugando a la muerte,
cual niño bárbaro. Él piensa
que ha de caer como rama que sobre las aguas flota,
antes de perderse, gota
de mar, en la mar inmensa.

En sueños oyó el acento de una palabra divina;
en sueños se le ha mostrado la cruda ley diamantina,
sin odio ni amor, y el frío
soplo del olvido sabe sobre un arenal de hastío.

Bajo las palmeras del oäsis el agua buena
miró brotar de la arena;
y se abrevó entre las dulces gacelas, y entre los fieros
animales carniceros . . .

Y supo cuánto es la vida hecha de sed y dolor.
Y fue compasivo para el ciervo y el cazador,
para el ladrón y el robado,
para el pájaro azorado,
para el sanguinario azor.

Con el sabio amargo dijo: Vanidad de vanidades,
todo es negra vanidad:
y oyó otra voz que clamaba, alma de sus soledades:
sólo eres tú, luz que fulges en el corazón, verdad.

Y viendo cómo lucían
miles de blancas estrellas,

90

XVIII
(The Poet)
For the book *The House of Springtime*
by Gregorio Martínez Sierra

Cursing his fate
like Glaucus, the sea god,
he looks, his pupil dim with weeping,
at the sea, which owes him its white virgin Scylla.

He knows that a stronger god,
like a barbaric child, is playing at death
with the immortal substance. He thinks
he will fall like a branch that floats on the water,
before he is lost, drop
of the sea, in the boundless sea.

In his dreams he heard the accent of a divine word;
in his dreams he was shown the cruel diamond-hard law,
without love or hate, and he knows
the cold breath of oblivion over a sandbank of boredom.

Under the palms of the oasis he watched
the good water well up from the sand;
and he quenched his thirst among the gentle gazelles
and among the fierce carnivores . . .

And he learned how much of life is made of thirst and pain.
And he was compassionate with the stag and the hunter,
with the robber and the robbed,
with the frightened bird
and the bloodthirsty hawk.

With the bitter sage he said: Vanity of vanities,
all is black vanity;
and he heard another voice, soul of his solitude, cry out:
you alone are truth, O light that glows in the heart.

And seeing how thousands
of white stars were shining,

pensaba que todas ellas
en su corazón ardían.
¡Noche de amor!
                    Y otra noche
sintió la mala tristeza
que enturbia la pura llama,
y el corazón que bosteza,
y el histrión que declama.

    Y dijo: las galerías
del alma que espera están
desiertas, mudas, vacías:
las blancas sombras se van.

    Y el demonio de los sueños abrió el jardín encantado
del ayer. ¡Cuán bello era!
¡Qué hermosamente el pasado
fingía la primavera,
cuando del árbol de otoño estaba el fruto colgado,
mísero fruto podrido,
que en el hueco acibarado
guarda el gusano escondido!

    ¡Alma, que en vano quisiste ser más joven cada día,
arranca tu flor, la humilde flor de la melancolía!

he thought they all were
aflame in his heart.
Night of love!
                    And another night
he felt the bad sorrow
that dims the pure flame,
and the heart that yawns,
and the playactor who declaims.

     And he said: the galleries
of the waiting soul are
deserted, silent, empty:
the white shadows depart.

And the demon of dreams opened the enchanted garden
of yesterday. How lovely it was!
How beautifully the past
feigned spring,
when the fruit hung from autumn's tree,
wretched rotten fruit,
which in the bitter hole
guards the hidden worm.

     O soul, that tried in vain to be younger each day,
pluck your flower, the humble flower of melancholy!

XIX

¡Verdes jardinillos,
claras plazoletas,
fuente verdinosa
donde el agua sueña,
donde el agua muda
resbala en la piedra! . . .

Las hojas de un verde
mustio, casi negras,
de la acacia, el viento
de septiembre besa,
y se lleva algunas
amarillas, secas,
jugando, entre el polvo
blanco de la tierra.

Linda doncellita,
que el cántaro llenas
de agua transparente,
tú, al verme, no llevas
a los negros bucles
de tu cabellera,
distraídamente,
la mano morena,
ni, luego, en el limpio
cristal te contemplas . . .

Tu miras al aire
de la tarde bella,
mientras de agua clara
el cántaro llenas.

XIX

Little green gardens,
small bright plazas,
greenish fountain
where the water dreams,
where the silent water
slips over the stone! . . .

The acacia leaves of
gloomy green, almost black,
kissed by the September wind
that carries some of them off,
yellow and dry,
to play in the white
dust of the earth.

Pretty little maid,
who fills her pitcher
with transparent water,
when you see me, you don't
raise your dark hand,
distractedly,
to the black ringlets
of your hair,
nor do you later observe
yourself in the limpid crystal . . .

You look at the air
of the lovely afternoon,
while with clear water
you fill the pitcher.

DEL CAMINO ✳ OF THE ROAD

XX
(Preludio)

Mientras la sombra pasa de un santo amor, hoy quiero
poner un dulce salmo sobre mi viejo atril.
Acordaré las notas del órgano severo
al suspirar fragante del pífano de abril.

Madurarán su aroma las pomas otoñales,
la mirra y el incienso salmodiarán su olor;
exhalarán su fresco perfume los rosales,
bajo la paz en sombra del tibio huerto en flor.

Al grave acorde lento de música y aroma,
la sola y vieja y noble razón de mi rezar
levantará su vuelo suave de paloma,
y la palabra blanca se elevará al altar.

XXI

Daba el reloj las doce . . . y eran doce
golpes de azada en tierra . . .
. . . ¡Mi hora!—grité— . . . El silencio
me respondió:—No temas;
tú no verás caer la última gota
que en la clepsidra tiembla.

Dormirás muchas horas todavía
sobre la orilla vieja,
y encontrarás una mañana pura
amarrada tu barca a otra ribera.

XX
(Prelude)

While the shadow of a sacred love passes, I wish today
to place a sweet psalm on my old music stand.
I will tune the notes of the severe organ
to the fragrant sighing of April's fife.

The autumn apples will their aroma ripen,
the myrrh and incense will sing their scented psalms;
the rose bushes will their fresh perfume exhale,
under the shady peace of the balmy orchard in bloom.

To the slow deep chord of music and aroma,
the sole and old and noble motive of my praying
will take its gentle dovelike flight,
and the white word to the altar will rise.

XXI

The clock was striking twelve . . . and they were
twelve strokes of the spade in the earth . . .
. . . "My hour!" I cried . . . Silence
answered me: "Fear not;
you will not see the last drop fall
that trembles in the water clock.

You will yet sleep many hours
upon the ancient shore,
and one pure morning you will find
your boat moored to the other bank."

XXII

Sobre la tierra amarga,
caminos tiene el sueño
laberínticos, sendas tortuosas,
parques en flor y en sombra y en silencio;

criptas hondas, escalas sobre estrellas;
retablos de esperanzas y recuerdos.
Figurillas que pasan y sonríen
—juguetes melancólicos de viejo—;

imágenes amigas,
a la vuelta florida del sendero,
y quimeras rosadas
que hacen camino . . . lejos . . .

XXIII

En la desnuda tierra del camino
la hora florida brota,
espino solitario,
del valle humilde en la revuelta umbrosa.

El salmo verdadero
de tenue voz hoy torna
al corazón, y al labio,
la palabra quebrada y temblorosa.

Mis viejos mares duermen; se apagaron
sus espumas sonoras
sobre la playa estéril. La tormenta
camina lejos en la nube torva.

Vuelve la paz al cielo;
la brisa tutelar esparce aromas
otra vez sobre el campo, y aparece,
en la bendita soledad, tu sombra.

XXII

Upon the bitter land,
dreaming has labyrinthine
roads, tortuous paths,
parks in bloom, and in shadow and in silence;

deep vaults, ladders to stars;
puppet stages of hopes and memories.
Little figures that pass by and smile
—an old man's melancholy toys—;

friendly images,
at the flowery bend in the path,
and rosy chimeras
that make their way . . . afar . . .

XXIII

On the naked earth of the road
the hour in bloom is born,
O solitary hawthorn,
in the shady turn of the humble valley.

The true psalm
of delicate voice today returns
to the heart, and to the lips,
the broken and tremulous word.

My old seas are asleep; their
sounding foam has subsided
on the sterile beach. Far away
the storm travels in the grim cloud.

Peace returns to the sky;
the tutelar breeze again scatters
aromas over the countryside, and,
in the blessed solitude, your shadow appears.

101

XXIV

El sol es un globo de fuego,
la luna es un disco morado.

Una blanca paloma se posa
en el alto ciprés centenario.

Los cuadros de mirtos parecen
de marchito velludo empolvado.

¡El jardín y la tarde tranquila! . . .
Suena el agua en la fuente de mármol.

XXV

¡Tenue rumor de túnicas que pasan
sobre la infértil tierra! . . .
¡Y lágrimas sonoras
de las campanas viejas!

Las ascuas mortecinas
del horizonte humean . . .
Blancos fantasmas lares
van enciendo estrellas.

—Abre el balcón. La hora
de una ilusión se acerca . . .
La tarde se ha dormido,
y las campanas sueñan.

XXIV

The sun is a globe of fire,
the moon is a violet disk.

A white dove alights
on the tall centenary cypress.

The beds of myrtle seem
like dusty faded velvet.

The garden and the tranquil afternoon! . . .
The water sounds in the marble fountain.

XXV

Faint rustle of tunics that pass
over the infertile land! . . .
And sonorous tears
of the old bells!

The dying embers
on the horizon are smoking . . .
White ghosts of household gods
are kindling stars.

"Open the balcony window. The hour
of an illusion draws near . . ."
The evening has fallen asleep,
and the bells are dreaming.

XXVI

¡Oh, figuras del atrio, más humildes
cada día y lejanas:
mendigos harapientos
sobre marmóreas gradas;

miserables ungidos
de eternidades santas,
manos que surgen de los mantos viejos
y de las rotas capas!

¿Pasó por vuestro lado
una ilusión velada,
de la mañana luminosa y fría
en las horas más plácidas? . . .

Sobre la negra túnica, su mano
era una rosa blanca . . .

XXVII

La tarde todavía
dará incienso de oro a tu plegaria,
y quizás el cenit de un nuevo día
amenguará tu sombra solitaria.

Mas no es tu fiesta el Ultramar lejano,
sino la ermita junto al manso río;
no tu sandalia el soñoliento llano
pisará, ni la arena del hastío.

Muy cerca está, romero,
la tierra verde y santa y florecida
de tus sueños; muy cerca, peregrino
que desdeñas la sombra del sendero
y el agua del mesón en tu camino.

XXVI

Oh, figures in the atrium, each day
more humble and more distant:
beggars in rags
on marble stairs;

miserable wretches annointed
with sacred eternities,
hands that emerge from old cloaks
and from torn capes!

Did there by your side
a veiled illusion pass
in the most placid hours
of a cold and luminous morning? . . .

On the black tunic, her hand
was a white rose . . .

XXVII

The afternoon will still
give golden incense to your prayer,
and perhaps the zenith of a new day
will diminish your lonely shadow.

But your fiesta is not the lands beyond the seas,
but the hermitage beside the gentle river;
your sandal will not tread the slumbering
plain, nor yet the sand of weariness.

Close at hand, O pilgrim, is
the green and sacred and flowering land
of your dreams; close at hand, O pilgrim
who scorns the shade on the path
and the water of the inn on your road.

XXVIII

Crear fiestas de amores
en nuestro amor pensamos,
quemar nuevos aromas
en montes no pisados,

y guardar el secreto
de nuestros rostros pálidos,
porque en las bacanales de la vida
vacías nuestras copas conservamos,

mientras con eco de cristal y espuma
ríen los zumos de la vida dorados.

.   .   .   .

Un pájaro escondido entre las ramas
del parque solitario,
silba burlón . . .
                          Nosotros exprimimos
la penumbra de un sueño en nuestro vaso . . .
Y algo, que es tierra en nuestra carne, siente
la humedad del jardín como un halago.

XXVIII

We intend to create festivals
of love affairs in our love,
to burn new aromas
on mountains yet untrod,

and to keep the secret
of our pale faces,
because in the bacchanalia of life
we keep our goblets empty,

while with echo of crystal and froth
the golden juices of the vine do laugh.

. . . .

A bird hidden among the branches
of the lonely park
utters a mocking whistle . . .
                           We squeeze
the shadow of a dream into our glass . . .
And something, which is earth in our flesh, feels
the dampness of the garden as a caress.

XXIX

Arde en tus ojos un misterio, virgen
esquiva y compañera.

No sé si es odio o es amor la lumbre
inagotable de tu aljaba negra.

Conmigo irás mientras proyecte sombra
mi cuerpo y quede a mi sandalia arena.

—Eres la sed o el agua en mi camino?
Dime, virgen esquiva y compañera.

XXX

Algunos lienzos del recuerdo tienen
luz de jardín y soledad de campo;
la placidez del sueño
en el paisaje familiar sonado.

Otros guardan las fiestas
de días aun lejanos;
figurillas sutiles
que pone un titerero en su retablo . . .

. . . .

Ante el balcón florido,
está la cita de un amor amargo.

Brilla la tarde en el resol bermejo . . .
La hiedra efunde de los muros blancos . . .

A la revuelta de una calle en sombra,
un fantasma irrisorio besa un nardo.

XXIX

A mystery burns in your eyes,
elusive virgin ever by my side.

I do not know whether the unquenchable fire
in your black quiver is hate or love.

With me you shall go so long as my body
casts a shadow and there is still sand for my sandal.

"Are you the thirst or the water along my way?
Tell me, elusive virgin ever by my side."

XXX

Of memory's canvases some have
garden light and country solitude;
the tranquility of a dream
in the dreamed-of familiar landscape.

Others preserve the fiestas
of days still far away;
delicate figurines
that a puppeteer puts upon his stage . . .

.   .   .   .

Before the flowery balcony,
is the rendezvous of a bitter love.

The afternoon sparkles in the red sun glare . . .
The ivy pours over the white walls . . .

At the bend of a shadowy street,
a derisive phantom kisses a purple nard.

XXXI

Crece en la plaza en sombra
el musgo, y en la piedra vieja y santa
de la iglesia. En el atrio hay un mendigo . . .
Más vieja que la iglesia tiene el alma.

Sube muy lento, en las mañanas frías,
por la marmórea grada,
hasta un rincón de piedra . . . Allí aparece
su mano seca entre la rota capa.

Con las órbitas huecas de sus ojos
ha visto cómo pasan
las blancas sombras, en los claros días,
las blancas sombras de las horas santas.

XXXII

Las ascuas de un crepúsculo morado
detrás del negro cipresal humean . . .
En la glorieta en sombra está la fuente
con su alado y desnudo Amor de piedra,
que sueña mudo. En la marmórea taza
reposa el agua muerta.

XXXI

Moss grows in the shade of the
plaza and on the old and sacred stone
of the church. In the atrium is a beggar . . .
Older than the church is his soul.

On cold mornings, he slowly climbs
the marble steps
to a stoney nook . . . There his dry hand
appears among the folds of his torn cape.

With the empty sockets of his eyes
he has seen how, on bright days,
the white shadows pass,
the white shadows of the holy hours.

XXXII

The embers of a purple twilight
behind the black cypress grove are smoking . . .
In the shaded arbor stands the fountain
with its winged and naked Cupid of stone,
silently dreaming. In the marble basin
the dead water rests.

XXXIII

¿Mi amor? . . . ¿Recuerdas, dime,
aquellos juncos tiernos,
lánguidos y amarillos
que hay en el cauce seco? . . .

¿Recuerdas la amapola
que calcinó el verano,
la amapola marchita,
negro crespón del campo? . . .

¿Te acuerdas del sol yerto
y humilde, en la mañana,
que brilla y tiembla roto
sobre una fuente helada? . . .

XXXIV

Me dijo un alba de la primavera:
Yo florecí en tu corazón sombrío
ha muchos años, caminante viejo
que no cortas las flores del camino.

Tu corazón de sombra, ¿acaso guarda
el viejo aroma de mis viejos lirios?
¿Perfuman aún mis rosas la alba frente
del hada de tu sueño adamantino?

Respondí a la mañana:
Sólo tienen cristal los sueños míos.
Yo no conozco el hada de mis sueños;
no sé si está mi corazón florido.

Pero si aguardas la mañana pura
que ha de romper el vaso cristalino,
quizás el hada te dará tus rosas,
mi corazón tus lirios.

XXXIII

My love? . . . Tell me, do you remember
those tender reeds,
languid and yellow,
that stand in the dry riverbed? . . .

Do you remember the poppy
the summer burned,
the withered poppy,
black crepe of the fields?

Do you recall the sun, cold
and humble, in the morning,
that glistens and trembles
broken on a frozen fountain?

XXXIV

A spring dawn said to me:
Many years ago I flowered
in your somber heart, old wayfarer
who doesn't cut the roadside flowers.

Your shadowed heart, does it keep perhaps
the old aroma of my old lilies?
Do my roses still perfume the candid brow
of the fairy of your diamond dream?

To the morning I replied:
My dreams hold only crystal.
I'm not acquainted with the fairy of my dreams
nor do I know whether my heart's in flower.

But if you await the pure morning
that is to break the crystal glass,
perhaps the fairy will give you your roses,
my heart, your lilies.

113

XXXV

Al borde del sendero un día nos sentamos.
Ya nuestra vida es tiempo, y nuestra sola cuita
son las desesperantes posturas que tomamos
para aguardar . . . Mas Ella no faltará a la cita.

XXXVI

Es una forma juvenil que un día
a nuestra casa llega.
Nosotros le decimos: ¿por qué tornas
a la morada vieja?
Ella abre la ventana, y todo el campo
en luz y aroma entra.
En el blanco sendero,
los troncos de los árboles negrean;
las hojas de sus copas
son humo verde que a lo lejos sueña.
Parece una laguna
el ancho río entre la blanca niebla
de la mañana. Por los montes cárdenos
camina otra quimera.

XXXV

We sit down one day by the side of the path.
Our life now is time and our only concern
is the maddening postures we assume
while we wait . . . But She'll not miss the rendezvous.

XXXVI

She is a youthful form that one day
comes to our house.
We say to her: Why do you return
to the old home? She opens the window,
and the whole countryside
in light and aroma comes in.
On the white path,
the trees look black;
the leaves of their crowns
are green smoke dreaming afar.
The wide river seems
like a pool in the white mist
of the morning. Through the purple
mountains, another chimera is walking.

115

XXXVII

¡Oh, dime, noche amiga, amada vieja,
que me traes el retablo de mis sueños
siempre desierto y desolado, y sólo
con mi fantasma dentro,
mi pobre sombra triste
sobe la estepa y bajo el sol de fuego,
o soñando amarguras
en las voces de todos los misterios,
dime, si sabes, vieja amada, dime
si son mías las lágrimas que vierto!
Me respondió la noche:
Jamás me revelaste tu secreto.
Yo nunca supe, amado,
si eras tú ese fantasma de tu sueño,
ni averigüé si era su voz la tuya,
o era la voz de un histrión grotesco.

Dije a la noche: Amada mentirosa,
tú sabes mi secreto;
tú has visto la honda gruta
donde fabrica su cristal mi sueño,
y sabes que mis lágrimas son mías,
y sabes mi dolor, mi dolor viejo.

¡Oh! Yo no sé, dijo la noche, amado,
yo no sé tu secreto,
aunque he visto vagar ese, que dices
desolado fantasma, por tu sueño.
Yo me asomo a las almas cuando lloran
y escucho su hondo rezo,
humilde y solitario,
ese que llamas salmo verdadero;

XXXVII

Oh, tell me, friendly night, old love
who brings me the puppet stage of my dreams
always empty and forlorn, and
with only my ghost inside,
my poor sad shadow
on the high plain and under a fiery sun,
or dreaming bitter dreams
in the voices of all mysteries,
tell me, if you know, old love, tell me
whether the tears I shed are my own.
The night answered me:
To me you never revealed your secret.
I never knew, my love,
whether you were that ghost of your dream,
nor did I ever find out whether his voice was yours,
or the voice of a grotesque buffoon.

I said to the night: O deceitful love,
you know my secret;
you have seen the deep grotto
where my dream its crystal makes,
and you know my tears are mine,
and you know my sorrow, my old sorrow.

Oh, said the night, I do not know, my love,
I do not know your secret,
although I have seen that ghost forlorn
of whom you speak, awandering through your dream.
I peer into souls when they weep
and listen to their deep prayer,
humble and lonely,
the prayer you call true psalm;

pero en las hondas bóvedas del alma
no sé si el llanto es una voz o un eco.

Para escuchar tu queja de tus labios
yo te busqué en tu sueño,
y allí te vi vagando en un borroso
laberinto de espejos.

but in the soul's deep vaults
I do not know whether the lament is voice or echo.

In order to listen to your complaint from your lips,
I sought you out in your dream,
and there I saw you wandering
in a cloudy maze of mirrors.

CANCIONES ✳ SONGS

XXXVIII

Abril florecía
frente a mi ventana.
Entre los jazmines
y las rosas blancas
de un balcón florido,
vi las dos hermanas.
La menor cosía,
la mayor hilaba . . .
Entre los jazmines
y las rosas blancas,
la más pequeñita,
risueña y rosada
—su aguja en el aire—
miró a mi ventana.

La mayor seguía,
silenciosa y pálida,
el huso en su rueca
que el lino enroscaba.
Abril florecía
frente a mi ventana.

Una clara tarde
la mayor lloraba,
entre los jazmines
y las rosas blancas,
y ante el blanco lino
que en su rueca hilaba.
—¿Qué tienes—le dije—
silenciosa pálida?
Señaló el vestido
que empezó la hermana.
En la negra túnica
la aguja brillaba;
sobre el blanco velo,
el dedal de plata.

XXXVIII

April was blooming
opposite my window.
Among the jasmine
and the white roses
on a flowery balcony,
I saw the two sisters.
The younger one was sewing,
the older one was spinning . . .
Among the jasmine
and the white roses,
the little one,
smiling and rosy
—her needle in the air—,
looked toward my window.

The older one went on,
silent and pale,
the spindle on her spinning wheel
that wound up the flax.
April was blooming
opposite my window.

One bright afternoon
the older one was crying,
among the jasmine
and the white roses,
and before the white flax
she was spinning on her wheel.
"What's the matter," I said to her,
"O pale and silent one?"
She pointed to the dress
her sister had begun.
On the black gown
the needle glinted;
on the white veil,
the silver thimble.

123

Señaló a la tarde
de abril que soñaba,
mientras que se oía
tañer de campanas.
Y en la clara tarde
me enseñó sus lágrimas . . .
Abril florecía
frente a mi ventana.

    Fue otro abril alegre
y otra tarde plácida.
El balcón florido
solitario estaba . . .
Ni la pequeñita
risueña y rosada,
ni la hermana triste,
silenciosa y pálida,
ni la negra túnica,
ni la toca blanca . . .
Tan sólo en el huso
el lino giraba
por mano invisible,
y en la oscura sala
la luna del limpio
espejo brillaba . . .
Entre los jazmines
y las rosas blancas
del balcón florido,
me miré en la clara
luna del espejo
que lejos soñaba . . .
Abril florecía
frente a mi ventana.

She pointed to the April
afternoon adreaming
while the ringing
of bells was heard.
And on the bright afternoon
she showed me her tears . . .
April was blooming
opposite my window.

It was another happy April
and another placid afternoon.
The flowery balcony
was deserted . . .
Neither the little one,
smiling and rosy,
nor the sad sister,
silent and pale,
nor the black gown,
nor the white headdress . . .
Only the flax
on the spindle was spun
by an invisible hand,
and in the dark living room
the plate glass of the clean
mirror was shining . . .
Among the jasmine
and the white roses
on the flowery balcony,
I looked at myself
in the clear glass of the mirror
that was dreaming afar . . .
April was blooming
opposite my window.

XXXIX
(Coplas elegíacas)

¡Ay del que llega sediento
a ver el agua correr,
y dice: la sed que siento
no me la calma el beber!

¡Ay de quien bebe y, saciada
la sed, desprecia la vida:
moneda al tahur prestada,
que sea al azar rendida!

Del iluso que suspira
bajo el orden soberano,
y del que sueña la lira
pitagórica en su mano.

¡Ay del noble peregrino
que se para a meditar,
después de largo camino,
en el horror de llegar!

¡Ay de la melancolía
que llorando se consuela,
y de la melomanía
de un corazón de zarzuela!

¡Ay de nuestro ruiseñor,
si en una noche serena
se cura del mal de amor
que llora y canta sin pena!

¡De los jardines secretos,
de los pensiles soñados,
y de los sueños poblados
de propósitos discretos!

¡Ay del galán sin fortuna
que ronda a la luna bella;

XXXIX
(Elegiac Verses)

Woe to him who thirsty comes
to see the water run,
and says: the thirst I feel
is not by drinking quenched!

Woe to him who drinks and,
when his thirst is slaked, despises life:
a coin to the gambler lent,
let it be to chance returned!

To the visionary who sighs
under the order supreme,
and to him who dreams the lyre
of Pythagoras in his hand.

Woe to the noble pilgrim
who stops to meditate,
the long journey over,
on the horror of arriving!

Woe to melancholy
that is consoled by tears,
and to the music madness
of a light-opera heart!

Woe to our nightingale,
if on a peaceful night
he's cured of love's affliction
that cries and sings without grief!

To the secret gardens,
the lovely gardens of our dreams,
and to the dreams inhabited
by discreet intentions!

Woe to the luckless lady's man
who courts the beautiful moon;

de cuantos caen de la luna,
de cuantos se marchan a ella!

¡De quien el fruto prendido
en la rama no alcanzó,
de quien el fruto ha mordido
y el gusto amargo probó!

¡Y de nuestro amor primero
y de su fe mal pagada,
y, también, del verdadero
amante de nuestra amada!

to all who fall from the moon,
to all who toward it depart!

    To him who failed to reach
the fruit hanging from the branch,
and to him who has bitten the fruit
and tried its bitter taste!

    And to our first love
and its ill-requited faith,
and also to the true
lover of our beloved!

XL
(Inventario galante)

Tus ojos me recuerdan
las noches de verano,
negras noches sin luna,
orilla al mar salado,
y el chispear de estrellas
del cielo negro y bajo.
Tus ojos me recuerdan
las noches de verano.
Y tu morena carne,
los trigos requemados,
y el suspirar de fuego
de los maduros campos.

Tu hermana es clara y débil
como los juncos lánguidos,
como los sauces tristes,
como los linos glaucos.
Tu hermana es un lucero
en el azul lejano . . .
Y es alba y aura fría
sobre los pobres álamos
que en las orillas tiemblan
del río humilde y manso.
Tu hermana es un lucero
en el azul lejano.

De tu morena gracia,
de tu soñar gitano,
de tu mirar de sombra
quiero llenar mi vaso.
Me embriagaré una noche
de cielo negro y bajo,
para cantar contigo,
orilla al mar salado,
una canción que deje

XL
(Gallant Inventory)

Your eyes remind me
of summer nights,
black moonless nights,
beside the salty sea,
and of the sparkle of stars
in the low black sky.
Your eyes remind me
of summer nights.
And your dark flesh,
the scorched wheat
and the sighing of fire
in the harvest fields.

Your sister is fair and frail
like the languid reeds,
like the sad willows,
like the light green flax.
Your sister is a morning
star in the distant blue . . .
And she is dawn and cold breeze
on the poor poplars
that tremble on the banks
of the humble and gentle river.
Your sister is a morning
star in the distant blue.

With your dark grace,
with your gypsy dreaming,
with your shadowy gaze
I want to fill my glass.
I will get drunk on
a night of low black sky,
to sing with you,
beside the salty sea,
a song that will leave

131

cenizas en los labios . . .
De tu mirar de sombra
quiero llenar mi vaso.

Para tu linda hermana
arrancaré los ramos
de florecillas nuevas
a los almendros blancos,
en un tranquilo y triste
alborear de marzo.
Los regaré con agua
de los arroyos claros,
los ataré con verdes
junquillos del remanso . . .
Para tu linda hermana
yo haré un ramito blanco.

ashes upon your lips . . .
With your shadowy gaze
I want to fill my glass.

   For your pretty sister
I will break branches
of little new blossoms
from the white almond trees
on a tranquil sad
dawning of March.
I will wash them with water
from the clear brooks,
I will tie them with little
green reeds from the pool . . .
For your pretty sister
I will make a white bouquet.

XLI

Me dijo una tarde
de la primavera:
Si buscas caminos
en flor en la tierra,
mata tus palabras
y oye tu alma vieja.
Que el mismo albo lino
que te viste, sea
tu traje de duelo,
tu traje de fiesta.
Ama tu alegría
y ama tu tristeza,
si buscas caminos
en flor en la tierra.
Respondí a la tarde
de la primavera:
Tú has dicho el secreto
que en mi alma reza:
yo odio la alegría
por odio a la pena.
Mas antes que pise
tu florida senda,
quisiera traerte
muerta mi alma vieja.

XLI

A spring afternoon
said to me:
If you seek roads
in flower on the land,
kill your words and
listen to your aged soul.
Let the same white linen
that clothes you be
your mourning suit,
your festive suit.
Love your happiness
and love your sorrow,
if you seek roads
in flower on the land.
I replied
to the spring afternoon:
You have told the secret
that runs in my soul:
I hate the happiness
for hate of the grief.
But before I tread
your flowery path,
I would like to bring you
my aged soul now dead.

XLII

La vida hoy tiene ritmo
de ondas que pasan,
de olitas temblorosas
que fluyen y se alcanzan.

La vida hoy tiene el ritmo de los ríos,
la risa de las aguas
que entre los verdes junquerales corren,
y entre las verdes cañas.

Sueño florido lleva el manso viento;
bulle la savia joven en las nuevas ramas;
tiemblan alas y frondas,
y la mirada sagital del águila
no encuentra presa . . . treme el campo en sueños,
vibra el sol como un arpa.

¡Fugitiva ilusión de ojos guerreros,
que por las selvas pasas
a la hora del cenit: tiemble en mi pecho
el oro de tu aljaba!

En tus labios florece la alegría
de tus campos en flor; tu veste alada
aroman las primeras velloritas,
las violetas perfuman tus sandalias.

Yo he seguido tus pasos en el viejo bosque,
arrebatados tras la corza rápida,
y los ágiles músculos rosados
de tus piernas silvestres entre las verdes ramas.

¡Pasajera ilusión de ojos guerreros
que por las selvas pasas
cuando la tierra reverdece y ríen
los ríos en las cañas!
¡Tiemble en mi pecho el oro
que llevas en tu aljaba!

136

XLII

Today life has a rhythm
of waves that pass,
of trembling wavelets
that flow and overtake each other.

Today life has the rhythm of rivers,
the laughter of the waters
that run among the green bulrushes
and among the green reeds.

The gentle wind carries a dream in flower;
the young sap stirs in the new branches,
wings and foliage tremble,
the arrowlike look of the eagle
finds no prey . . . The dreaming countryside shivers,
the sun vibrates like a harp.

Fugitive illusion with warlike eyes,
you who through the forests pass
at the zenith hour: let the gold
from your quiver tremble in my breast!

On your lips there flowers the joy
of your fields in bloom; your winged garments
are scented by the first cowslips,
violets perfume your sandals.

Through the old woods I have followed your steps,
swept along by the swift doe,
and the agile pink muscles
of your sylvan legs among the green branches.

Fleeting illusion with warlike eyes,
you who through the forests pass
when the earth grows green again and
the rivers laugh among the reeds!
Let the gold you carry in your quiver
tremble in my breast!

XLIII

Era una mañana y abril sonreía.
Frente al horizonte dorado moría
la luna, muy blanca y opaca; tras ella,
cual tenue ligera quimera, corría
la nube que apenas enturbia una estrella.

. . . .

Como sonreía la rosa mañana
al sol del oriente abrí mi ventana;
y en mi triste alcoba penetró el oriente
en canto de alondras, en risa de fuente
y en suave perfume de flora temprana.

Fue una clara tarde de melancolía.
Abril sonreía. Yo abrí las ventanas
de mi casa al viento . . . El viento traía
perfume de rosas, doblar de campanas . . .

Doblar de campanas lejanas, llorosas,
suave de rosas aromado aliento . . .
. . . ¿Dónde están los huertos floridos de rosas?
¿Qué dicen las dulces campanas al viento?

. . . .

Pregunté a la tarde de abril que moría:
¿Al fin la alegría se acerca a mi casa?
La tarde de abril sonrió: La alegría
pasó por tu puerta—luego, sombría:
Pasó por tu puerta. Dos veces no pasa.

XLIII

It was morning and April was smiling.
Facing the golden horizon, the moon
was dying, all white and opaque; behind it,
like a faint swift chimera, ran
the cloud that barely obscures a star.

.   .   .   .

As the rosy morning was smiling
at the eastern sun, I opened my window;
and into my sad bedroom the east wind entered
in lark song, in fountain laughter
and in soft perfume of early flowers.

It was a bright melancholy afternoon.
April was smiling. I opened the windows
of my house to the wind . . . The wind
brought perfume of roses, tolling of bells . . .

Tolling of distant, weeping bells,
soft breath scented with roses . . .
. . . Where are the gardens with roses in bloom?
What do the sweet bells say to the wind?

.   .   .   .

I asked the dying April afternoon:
Is happiness approaching my house at last?
The April afternoon smiled: Happiness
passed your door—and then, somberly:
It passed your door. Twice it does not pass.

139

XLIV

El casco roído y verdoso
del viejo falucho
reposa en la arena . . .
La vela tronchada parece
que aun sueña en el sol y en el mar.

El mar hierve y canta . . .
El mar es un sueño sonoro
bajo el sol de abril.
El mar hierve y ríe
con olas azules y espumas de leche y de plata,
el mar hierve y ríe
bajo el cielo azul.
El mar lactescente,
el mar rutilante,
que ríe en sus liras de plata sus risas azules . . .
¡Hierve y ríe el mar!

El aire parece que duerme encantado
en la fúlgida niebla de sol blanquecino.
La gaviota palpita en el aire dormido, y al lento
volar soñoliento, se aleja y se pierde en la bruma del sol.

XLIV

The corroded and greenish hull
of the old felucca
rests on the sand . . .
The torn sail still seems
to dream of the sun and the sea.

The sea boils and sings . . .
The sea is a sounding dream
under the April sun.
The sea boils and laughs
with blue waves and spume of milk and silver,
the sea boils and laughs
under the blue sky.
The milky sea,
the sparkling sea,
that laughs its blue laughter on its silver lyres.
The sea boils and laughs!

The wind seems to sleep bewitched
in the bright fog of whitish sunshine.
The seagull flaps in the sleeping wind and its slow
drowsy flight recedes and is lost in the sun-lit mist.

XLV

El sueño bajo el sol que aturde y ciega,
tórrido sueño en la hora del arrebol;
el río luminoso el aire surca;
esplende la montaña;
la tarde es polvo y sol.

El sibilante caracol del viento
ronco dormita en el remoto alcor;
emerge el sueño ingrave en la palmera,
luego se enciende en el naranjo en flor.

La estúpida cigüeña
su garabato escribe en el sopor
del molino parado; el toro abate
sobre la hierba la testuz feroz.

La verde, quieta espuma del ramaje
efunde sobre el blanco paredón,
lejano, inerte, del jardín sombrío,
dormido bajo el cielo fanfarrón.

. . . .

Lejos, enfrente de la tarde roja,
refulge el ventanal del torreón.

. . . .

XLV

The dream under the sun that dazzles and blinds,
torrid dream at the hour of sunset red;
the wind furrows the luminous river;
the mountain splendors;
the afternoon is dust and sun.

The sibilant sea shell of the raucous
wind dozes on a remote hilltop;
the dream emerges weightless on the palm tree,
then flames on the orange tree in bloom.

The stupid stork scrawls
its pothook on the torpor
of the motionless windmill; the bull
lowers his fierce head over the grass.

The green still foam of the foliage,
distant, inert, pours over the thick
white wall of the shady garden
asleep under a show-off sky.

.   .   .   .

In the distance, facing the red afternoon,
glitters the great window of the tower.

.   .   .   .

HUMORISMOS, FANTASÍAS, APUNTES

✳ HUMORS, FANTASIES, JOTTINGS

Los Grandes Inventos

XLVI

(La noria)

La tarde caía
triste y polvorienta.

El agua cantaba
su copla plebeya
en los cangilones
de la noria lenta.

Soñaba la mula,
¡pobre mula vieja!
al compás de sombra
que en el agua suena.

La tarde caía
triste y polvorienta.

Yo no sé que noble,
divino poeta,
unió a la amargura
de la eterna rueda

la dulce armonía
del agua que sueña,
y vendó tus ojos,
¡pobre mula vieja! . . .

Mas sé que fue un noble,
divino poeta,
corazón maduro
de sombra y de ciencia.

The Great Inventions

XLVI
(The Noria)

The afternoon was drawing
to a close, sad and dusty.

The water was singing
its plebeian song
in the buckets
of the slow noria.

The mule was dreaming,
poor old mule!
to the shadow beat
of the sounding water.

The afternoon was drawing
to a close, sad and dusty.

I do not know what noble,
divine poet
linked to the bitterness
of the eternal round

the sweet harmony
of the dreaming water,
and bound your eyes,
poor old mule! . . .

But I know it was a noble,
divine poet,
a heart ripe
with shadow and learning.

XLVII
(El cadalso)

La aurora asomaba
lejana y siniestra.

El lienzo de Oriente
sangraba tragedias,
pintarrajeadas
con nubes grotescas.

. . . .

En la vieja plaza
de una vieja aldea,
erguía su horrible
pavura esquelética
el tosco patíbulo
de fresca madera . . .

La aurora asomaba
lejana y siniestra.

XLVII
(The Gallows)

Dawn was breaking
distant and sinister.

The canvas of the East
was bleeding tragedies
daubed
with grotesque clouds.

. . . .

In the old plaza
of an old village,
the rough scaffold
of fresh wood
raised its horrible
skeletal terror . . .

Dawn was breaking
distant and sinister.

XLVIII
(Las moscas)

Vosotras, las familiares,
inevitables golosas,
vosotras, moscas vulgares,
me evocáis todas las cosas.

¡Oh, viejas moscas voraces
como abejas en abril,
viejas moscas pertinaces
sobre mi calva infantil!

¡Moscas del primer hastío
en el salón familiar,
las claras tardes de estío
en que yo empecé a soñar!

Y en la aborrecida escuela,
raudas moscas divertidas,
perseguidas
por amor de lo que vuela,

—que todo es volar—sonoras,
rebotando en los cristales
en los días otoñales . . .
Moscas de todas las horas,

de infancia y adolescencia,
de mi juventud dorada;
de esta segunda inocencia,
que da en no creer en nada,

de siempre . . . Moscas vulgares,
que de puro familiares
no tendréis digno cantor:
yo sé que os habéis posado

sobre el juguete encantado,
sobre el librote cerrado,
sobre la carta de amor,

XLVIII
(Flies)

Familiar flies,
unavoidable, gluttonous,
everyday flies,
to me you evoke all things.

Old flies as ravenous
as bees in April,
persistent old flies
on my infant bald head!

Flies of my first boredom
in the family living room,
on the bright summer afternoons
when I began to dream!

And in the hated school,
amusing swift flies,
pursued
for love of what flies,

—for flying is what counts—
sounding, bouncing against
the window panes on autumn days . . .
Flies of all seasons,

of childhood and adolescence,
of my golden youth;
of this second innocence,
that takes to believing in nothing,

of now and forever . . . Common flies,
so utterly familiar
that you'll not have a worthy singer:
I know that you have settled

on the enchanted toy,
on the big unopened book,
on the love letter,

151

sobre los párpados yertos
de los muertos.

Inevitables golosas,
que ni labráis como abejas,
ni brilláis como mariposas;
pequeñitas, revoltosas,
vosotras, amigas viejas,
me evocáis todas las cosas.

XLIX
(Elegía de un madrigal)

Recuerdo que una tarde de soledad y hastío,
¡oh tarde como tantas!, el alma mía era,
bajo el azul monótono, un ancho y terso río
que ni tenía un pobre juncal en su ribera.

¡Oh mundo sin encanto, sentimental inopia
que borra el misterioso azoge del cristal!
¡Oh el alma sin amores que el Universo copia
con un irremediable bostezo universal!

✻

Quiso el poeta recordar a solas,
las ondas bien amadas, la luz de los cabellos
que él llamaba en sus rimas rubias olas.
Leyó . . . La letra mata: no se acordaba de ellos . . .

Y un día—como tantos—al aspirar un día
aromas de una rosa que en el rosal se abría,
brotó como una llama la luz de los cabellos
que él en sus madrigales llamaba rubias olas,
brotó, porque un aroma igual tuvieron ellos . . .
Y se alejó en silencio para llorar a solas.

152

on the rigid eyelids
of the dead.

Unavoidable, gluttonous flies,
that neither work like bees,
nor glitter like butterflies;
diminutive and pesky,
old friends
to me you evoke all things.

XLIX
(Elegy for a Madrigal)

I remember that one lonely, weary afternoon,
oh afternoon like so many! my soul, under
the monotonous blue, was a broad smooth river
without so much as a patch of reeds on its bank.

Oh world without charm, so destitute of feeling
that it effaces the mirror's mysterious quicksilver!
Oh loveless soul that the Universe copies
with an incurable universal yawn!

✳

The poet tried to remember in solitude
the well-loved waves, the light of her hair
that in his poems he called golden waves.
He read . . . The letter kills: he couldn't remember them . . .

And one day—like so many others—one day on breathing
the fragrance of a rose opening on the rosebush,
there burst forth like a flame the light of her hair
that in his madrigals he called golden waves,
it burst forth because they had that same fragrance . . .
And he withdrew in silence to lonely tears.

153

L

(Acaso . . .)

Como atento no más a mi quimera
no reparaba en torno mío, un día
me sorprendió la fértil primavera
que en todo el ancho campo sonreía.

Brotaban verdes hojas
de las hinchadas yemas del ramaje,
y flores amarillas, blancas, rojas,
alegraban la mancha del paisaje.

Y era una lluvia de saetas de oro,
el sol sobre las frondas juveniles;
del amplio río en el caudal sonoro
se miraban los álamos gentiles.

Tras de tanto camino es la primera
vez que miro brotar la primavera,
dije, y después, declamatoriamente:

—¡Cuán tarde ya para la dicha mía!—
Y luego, al caminar, como quien siente
alas de otra ilusión:—Y todavía
¡yo alcanzaré mi juventud un día!

L
(Perhaps . . .)

As, attentive only to my fancy,
I paid no heed to my surroundings,
I was surprised one day by fertile spring,
which in the whole broad countryside was smiling.

Green leaves were sprouting
from the branches' swollen buds
and flowers, yellow, white, and red,
made gay the patch of landscape.

And the sun on the young foliage
was a rain of golden arrows;
and in the sonorous flow of the broad river
the graceful poplars gazed at themselves.

After so much wayfaring, it is the first
time I have seen spring burst forth,
I said, and then in declamatory style:

"How late now for my happiness!"
And then, on walking on, as one who feels
wings of new illusion: "And yet,
I will overtake my youth one day!"

LI
(Jardín)

Lejos de tu jardín quema la tarde
inciensos de oro en purpurinas llamas,
tras el bosque de cobre y de ceniza.
En tu jardín hay dalias.
¡Malhaya tu jardín! . . . Hoy me parece
la obra de un peluquero,
con esa pobre palmerilla enana,
y ese cuadro de mirtos recortados . . .
y el naranjito en su tonel . . . El agua
de la fuente de piedra
no cesa de reír sobre la concha blanca.

LI
(Garden)

Far from your garden the afternoon
burns golden incense in purple flames,
beyond the woods of copper and ashes.
In your garden there are dahlias.
Damned be your garden! . . . Today it seems
to me the work of a hairdresser,
with that poor little dwarf palm,
and that bed of cut-back myrtles . . .
and the little orange tree in its barrel . . .
The water in the stone fountain
laughs ceaselessly above its white shell.

LII

(Fantasía de una noche de abril)

¿Sevilla? . . . ¿Granada? . . . La noche de luna.
Angosta la calle, revuelta y moruna,
de blancas paredes y obscuras ventanas.
Cerrados postigos, corridas persianas . . .
El cielo vestía su gasa de abril.

Un vino risueño me dijo el camino.
Yo escucho los áureos consejos del vino,
que el vino es a veces escala de ensueño.
Abril y la noche y el vino risueño
cantaron en coro su salmo de amor.

La calle copiaba, con sombra en el muro,
el paso fantasma y el sueño maduro
de apuesto embozado, galán caballero:
espada tendida, calado sombrero . . .
La luna vertía su blanco soñar.

Como un laberinto mi sueño torcía
de calle en calleja. Mi sombra seguía
de aquel laberinto la sierpe encantada,
en pos de una oculta plazuela cerrada.
La luna lloraba su dulce blancor.

La casa y la clara ventana florida,
de blancos jazmines y nardos prendida,
más blancos que el blanco soñar de la luna . . .
—Señora, la hora, tal vez importuna . . .
¿Que espere? (La dueña se lleva el candil.)

Ya sé que sería quimera, señora,
mi sombra galante buscando a la aurora
en noches de estrellas y luna, si fuera
mentira la blanca nocturna quimera
que usurpa a la luna su trono de luz.

LII
(Fantasy of an April Night)

Seville? . . . Granada? . . . The moonlit night.
Narrow the street, twisting and Moorish,
with white walls and windows dark.
Posterns shut, shutters closed . . .
The sky was wearing its April gauze.

A laughing wine told me the way.
I listen to the golden advice of wine,
for wine is at times a ladder to dreams.
April and the night and the laughing wine
sang in chorus their psalm of love.

The street copies, with shadow on the wall,
the phantom pace and mature dream
of an elegant gentleman, muffled and gallant:
his sword at his side, his hat pulled down . . .
The moon poured down its dreamy white.

Like a labyrinth my dream twisted
from street to alley. My shadow followed
the enchanted serpent of that labyrinth,
in search of a little plaza, hidden and closed.
The moon wept its soft whiteness.

The house and the bright flowery window,
with white jasmine and spikenards adorned,
whiter than the white dreaming of the moon . . .
"Milady, the ill-timed hour perhaps . . .
I should wait? (The duenna carries off the lamp.)

I know, milady, that my gallant shadow
seeking the dawn on a moon- and starlit night
would be mere fantasy if the white
nocturnal fantasy that usurps
the moon's throne of light were a lie.

159

¡Oh dulce señora, más cándida y bella
que la solitaria matutina estrella
tan clara en el cielo! ¿Por qué silenciosa
oís mi nocturna querella amorosa?
¿Quién hizo, señora, cristal vuestra voz?

La blanca quimera parece que sueña.
Acecha en la oscura estancia la dueña.
—Señora, si acaso otra sombra emboscada
teméis, en la sombra, fiad en mi espada . . .
Mi espada se ha visto a la luna brillar.

¿Acaso os parece mi gesto anacrónico?
El vuestro es, señora, sobrado lacónico.
¿Acaso os asombra mi sombra embozada,
de espada tendida y toca plumada? . . .
¿Seréis la cautiva del moro Gazul? . . .

Dijéraislo, y pronto mi amor os diría
el son de mi guzla y la algarabía
más dulce que oyera ventana moruna.
Mi guzla os dijera la noche de luna,
la noche de cándida luna de abril.

Dijera la clara cantiga de plata
del patio moruno, y la serenata
que lleva el aroma de floridas preces
a los miradores y a los ajimeces,
los salmos de un blanco fantasma lunar.

Dijera las danzas de trenzas lascivas,
las muelles cadencias de ensueños, las vivas
centellas de lánguidos rostros velados,
los tibios perfumes, los huertos cerrados;
dijera el aroma letal del harén.

Yo guardo, señora, en viejo salterio
también una copla de blanco misterio,
la copla más suave, más dulce y más sabia

O sweet lady, whiter and more beautiful
than the solitary morning star
so bright in the sky. Why in silence
do you hear my nocturnal plaint of love?
Who, milady, turned your voice to crystal?"

The white fantasy appears to dream.
The duenna lurks in the dark room.
"Milady, if perhaps in the shadow
you fear another hidden shadow, trust
my sword. It has been seen in the moonlight to flash.

Perhaps to you my posture seems out-of-date?
Yours, milady, is excessively laconic.
Maybe you're astonished by my muffled shadow,
with girded sword and feathered hat?
Are you, I wonder, the captive of the Moor Gazul?

Say you so, and my love would tell you
the sound of my rebec and the sweetist Arabic
that ever Moorish window heard.
My rebec would tell you of the moonlit night,
the night of April's candid moon.

It would tell of the clear silver song
of the Moorish patio, and of the serenade
that carries the aroma of special glories
to the balconies and arched windows,
of the psalms of a white lunar phantom.

It would tell of the dances of lascivious tresses,
the soft rhythms of dreams, the quick
flashes in languid veiled faces,
the tepid perfumes, the closed gardens;
it would tell of the mortal aroma of the harem.

I also keep, milady, in an old psalter,
a poem of white mystery,
the gentlest, sweetest and wisest verses

que evoca las claras estrellas de Arabia
y aromas de un moro jardín andaluz.

Silencio . . . En la noche la paz de la luna
alumbra la blanca ventana muruna.
Silencio . . . Es el musgo que brota, y la hiedra
que lento desgarra la tapia de piedra . . .
El llanto que vierte la luna de abril.

—Si sois una sombra de la primavera
blanca entre jazmines, o antigua quimera
soñada en las trovas de dulces cantores,
yo soy una sombra de viejos cantares,
y el signo de un álgebra vieja de amores.

Los gayos, lascivos decires mejores,
los árabes albos nocturnos soñares,
las coplas mundanas, los salmos talares,
poned en mis labios;
yo soy una sombra también del amor.

Ya muerta la luna, mi sueño volvía
por la retorcida, moruna calleja.
El sol en Oriente reía
su risa más vieja.

that evoke the bright stars of Arabia
and the aromas of an Andalusian Moorish garden."

Silence . . . In the night the lunar peace
lights the white Moorish window.
Silence . . . It's the sprouting moss and the ivy
that slowly cracks the wall of stone . . .
The tears shed by the April moon.

"If you are a shadow of white spring
among the jasmine, or an ancient fantasy
dreamed in the gentle troubadours' verses,
I am a shadow of old songs
and the sign of an old algebra of loves.

Put on my lips
the best gay, lascivious sayings,
the Arabic white nocturnal dreamings,
the worldly verses, the priestly psalms;
I am also a shadow of love."

The moon now extinguished, my dream
turned back through the twisting Moorish alley.
The sun in the East laughed
its old, old laugh.

163

LIII

(A un naranjo y a un limonero)
Vistos en una Tienda de Plantas y Flores

Naranjo en maceta, ¡qué triste es tu suerte!
Medrosas tiritan tus hojas menguadas.
Naranjo en la corte, qué pena da verte
con tus naranjitas secas y arrugadas!

Pobre limonero de fruto amarillo
cual pomo pulido de pálida cera,
¡qué pena mirarte, mísero arbolillo
criado en mezquino tonel de madera!

De los claros bosques de la Andalucía,
¿quién os trajo a esta castellana tierra
que barren los vientos de la adusta sierra,
hijos de los campos de la tierra mía?

¡Gloria de los huertos, árbol limonero,
que enciendes los frutos de pálido oro,
y alumbras del negro cipresal austero
las quietas plegarias erguidas en coro;

y fresco naranjo del patio querido,
del campo risueño y el huerto soñado,
siempre en mi recuerdo maduro o florido
de frondas y aromas y frutos cargado!

LIII

(To an Orange Tree and a Lemon Tree)
Seen in a Plant and Flower Store

Orange tree in a flower pot, how sad is your fate!
Your withered leaves shiver with fear.
Orange tree in Madrid, what sorrow to see you
with your little oranges, dry and wrinkled!

Poor lemon tree with yellow fruit
like polished apples of pale wax,
what sorrow to look at you, wretched little tree,
raised in a miserable wooden barrel!

From the bright green groves of Andalusia,
who brought you, children of my native
land, to this Castilian plain
swept by the winds of the grim sierra?

Glory of the orchards, O lemon tree,
kindling your pale golden fruit,
and illuminating the quiet prayers
of the stern black cypresses in chorus raised;

and fresh orange tree of the beloved patio,
of the smiling countryside and the orchard of my dreams,
always in my memory, ripe or in flower,
laden with fronds and aromas and fruit!

LIV

(Los sueños malos)

Está la plaza sombría;
muere el día.
Suenan lejos las campanas.

De balcones y ventanas
se iluminan las vidrieras,
con reflejos mortecinos,
como huesos blanquecinos,
y borrosas calaveras.

En toda la tarde brilla
una luz de pesadilla.
Está el sol en el ocaso.
Suena el eco de mi paso.

—¿Eres tú? ya te esperaba . . .
—No eras tú a quien yo buscaba.

LIV
(Bad Dreams)

The plaza is shadowed;
the day is dying.
Bells sound in the distance.

Of balconies and windows
the panes of glass light up,
with dying reflections,
like whitish bones
and half-seen skulls.

The whole evening glows
with a nightmarish light.
The sun stands in the West.
The echo of my step resounds.

"Is it you? I was waiting for you . . ."
"You're not the one I was looking for."

LV
(Hastío)

Pasan las horas de hastío
por la estancia familiar,
el amplio cuarto sombrío
donde yo empecé a soñar.

Del reloj arrinconado,*
que en la penumbra clarea,
el tic-tac acompasado
odiosamente golpea.

Dice la monotonía
del agua clara al caer:
un día es como otro día;
hoy es lo mismo que ayer.

Cae la tarde. El viento agita
el parque mustio y dorado . . .
¡Qué largamente ha llorado
toda la fronda marchita!

Arrinconado may mean "cornered" in the sense that a threatening animal may be said to be cornered. Conceivably this clock is felt to be vaguely threatening.

LV
(Weariness)

The weary hours pass by
in the family living room,
the somber, spacious room
where I began to dream.

From the cornered clock,
which in shadow clearly shows,
the rhythmic tick-tock
keeps its odious beat.

Says the monotony
of the clear water as it falls:
one day is like another;
today is the same as yesterday.

Evening falls. The wind agitates
the withered park of golden hue . . .
How long has all the
faded foliage wept!

LVI

Sonaba el reloj la una,
dentro de mi cuarto. Era
triste la noche. La luna,
reluciente calavera,

ya del cenit declinando,
iba del ciprés del huerto
fríamente iluminando
el alto ramaje yerto.

Por la entreabierta ventana
llegaban a mis oídos
metálicos alaridos
de una música lejana.

Una música tristona,
una mazurca olvidada,
entre inocente y burlona,
mal tañida y mal soplada.

Y yo sentí el estupor
del alma cuando bosteza,
el corazón, la cabeza,
y . . . morirse es lo mejor.

LVI

The clock was striking one
inside my room. The night
was sad. The moon,
a shining skull,

already falling from its zenith,
was coldly lighting up
the tall stiff branches
of the cypress in the garden.

Through the half-opened window
there reached my ears
shrill metallic sounds
of a distant music.

A sad old music,
a forgotten mazurka,
between innocent and mocking,
badly strummed and badly blown.

And I felt the stupor
of the soul when the heart
yawns, the head
and . . . to die is best.

LVII
(Consejos)

I

Este amor que quiere ser
acaso pronto será;
pero ¿cuándo ha de volver
lo que acaba de pasar?

Hoy dista mucho de ayer.
¡Ayer es Nunca jamás!

II

Moneda que está en la mano
quizá se debe guardar;
la monedita del alma
se pierde si no se da.

LVII
(Advice)

I

This love that tries to be
will perhaps soon be;
but when will what's past
and gone come back again?

Today is far from yesterday.
Yesterday is nevermore.

II

A coin in the hand
should perhaps be saved;
the soul's little coin
is lost if not given.

173

LVIII
(Glosa)

Nuestras vidas son los ríos
que van a dar a la mar,
que es el morir. ¡Gran cantar!

Entre los poetas míos
tiene Manrique un altar.

Dulce goce de vivir:
mala ciencia del pasar,
ciego huir a la mar.

Tras el pavor del morir
está el placer de llegar.

¡Gran placer!
Mas ¿y el horror de volver?
¡Gran pesar!

LVIII
(Gloss)

Our lives are the rivers
that go to meet the sea,
which is death. Great poem!

Among my poets
Manrique has an altar.

Sweet enjoyment of living:
bad science of passing away,
blind flight to the sea.

After the dread of dying
is the pleasure of arriving.

Great pleasure!
But, the horror of returning?
Great sorrow!

LIX

Anoche cuando dormía
soñé, ¡bendita ilusión!,
que una fontana fluía
dentro de mi corazón.
Di, ¿por qué acequia escondida,
agua, vienes hasta mí,
manantial de nueva vida
en donde nunca bebí?

Anoche cuando dormía
soñé, ¡bendita ilusión!,
que una colmena tenía
dentro de mi corazón;
y las doradas ovejas
iban fabricando en él,
con las amarguras viejas,
blanca cera y dulce miel.

Anoche cuando dormía
soñé, ¡bendita ilusión!
que un ardiente sol lucía
dentro de mi corazón.
Era ardiente porque daba
calores de rojo hogar,
y era sol porque alumbraba
y porque hacía llorar.

Anoche cuando dormía
soñé, ¡bendita ilusión!,
que era Dios lo que tenía
dentro de mi corazón.

LIX

Last night when I was asleep
I dreamt, blessed illusion!,
that a fountain was flowing
within my heart.
Tell me, O water, by what hidden
channel you come to me,
wellspring of new life
from which I never drank?

Last night when I was asleep
I dreamt, blessed illusion!,
that I had a beehive
within my heart;
and in it the golden bees
were elaborating
with old and bitter things,
white wax and honey sweet.

Last night when I was asleep
I dreamt, blessed illusion!,
that a fiery sun was shining
within my heart.
It was fiery because it gave
off hearth-red heat,
and it was a sun because
it shed light and made one weep.

Last night when I was asleep
I dreamt, blessed illusion!,
that God was what I held
within my heart.

177

LX

¿Mi corazón se ha dormido?
Colmenares de mis sueños
¿ya no labráis? ¿Está seca
la noria del pensamiento,
los cangilones vacíos,
girando, de sombra llenos?

No, mi corazón no duerme.
Está despierto, despierto.
Ni duerme ni sueña, mira,
los claros ojos abiertos,
señas lejanas y escucha
a orillas del gran silencio.

LX

    Has my heart fallen asleep?
Beehives of my dreams,
do you work no more? Has
the noria of my thought run dry,
the empty water-buckets
revolving, full of shadow?

    No, my heart sleeps not.
It is awake, awake.
It neither sleeps, nor dreams, it watches
distant signs, its clear eyes open,
and listens on the shores
of the great silence.

GALERÍAS ✳ GALLERIES

LXI
(Introducción)

Leyendo un claro día
mis bien amados versos,
he visto en el profundo
espejo de mis sueños

que una verdad divina
temblando está de miedo,
y es una flor que quiere
echar su aroma al viento.

El alma del poeta
se orienta hacia el misterio.
Sólo el poeta puede
mirar lo que está lejos
dentro del alma, en turbio
y mago sol envuelto.

En esas galerías,
sin fondo, del recuerdo,
donde las pobres gentes
colgaron cual trofeo

el traje de una fiesta
apolillado y viejo,
allí el poeta sabe
el laborar eterno
mirar de las doradas
abejas de los sueños.

Poetas, con el alma
atenta al hondo cielo,
en la cruel batalla
o en el tranquilo huerto,

la nueva miel labramos
con los dolores viejos,
la veste blanca y pura

LXI
(Introduction)

Reading one bright day
my well-loved verses,
I saw in the profound
mirror of my dreams

a divine truth
trembling with fear,
and it's a flower that wants
to cast its aroma on the wind.

The poet's soul
is oriented to mystery.
Only the poet can
contemplate what's distant
within the soul, in misty,
magical sunlight enveloped.

In those endless
galleries of memory,
where the poor folks
hung like a trophy

the gala dress,
moth-eaten and old,
there the poet knows
how to watch the eternal
working of the golden
bees of dreams.

We poets, with our souls
attentive to the deep sky,
in the cruel battle
or in the tranquil garden,

new honey create
with sorrows old,
the pure white robe

183

pacientemente hacemos,
y bajo el sol bruñimos
el fuerte arnés de hierro.

El alma que no sueña,
el enemigo espejo,
proyecta nuestra imagen
con un perfil grotesco.

Sentimos una ola
de sangre, en nuestro pecho,
que pasa . . . y sonreímos,
y a laborar volvemos.

we patiently make,
and burnish under the sun
our strong armor of iron.

The enemy mirror,
the soul that doesn't dream,
projects our image
with a grotesque profile.

In our breast
we feel a surge of blood
that passes . . . and we smile
and to our work return.

LXII

Desgarrada la nube, el arco iris
brillando ya en el cielo,
y en un fanal de lluvia
y sol el campo envuelto.

Desperté. ¿Quién enturbia
los mágicos cristales de mi sueño?
Mi corazón latía
atónito y disperso.

. . . ¡El limonar florido,
el cipresal del huerto,
el prado verde, el sol, el agua, el iris . . .
¡el agua en tus cabellos! . . .

Y todo en la memoria se perdía
como una pompa de jabón al viento.

LXII

The riven cloud, the rainbow
already shining in the sky,
and the countryside enveloped
in a bright mantle* of rain and sun.

I awoke. Who beclouds
the magic windows of my dreams?
My heart was beating
astonished and unfocused.

. . . The lemon grove in flower,
the cypresses in the garden,
the green meadow, the sun, the water, the iris! . . .
the water on your hair! . . .

And everything in my memory was lost
like a soap bubble in the wind.

*I use "mantle" here in the sense of a lacy hood or sheath that gives light by incandescence when placed over a flame. Everybody knew about this kind of "mantle" in the age of gaslights.

187

LXIII

Y era el demonio de mi sueño, el ángel
más hermoso. Brillaban
como aceros los ojos victoriosos,
y las sangrientas llamas
de su antorcha alumbraron
la honda cripta del alma.

—¿Vendrás conmigo?—No, jamás; las tumbas
y los muertos me espantan.
Pero la férrea mano
mi diestro atenazaba.

—Vendrás conmigo . . . Y avancé en mi sueño,
cegado por la roja luminaria.
Y en la cripta sentí sonar cadenas,
y rebullir de fieras enjauladas.

LXIV

Desde el umbral de un sueño me llamaron . . .
Era la buena voz, la voz querida.

—Dime: ¿vendrás conmigo a ver el alma? . . .
Llegó a mi corazón una caricia.

—Contigo siempre . . . Y avancé en mi sueño
por una larga, escueta galería,
sintiendo el roce de la veste pura
y el palpitar suave de la mano amiga.

LXIII

And it was the demon of my dreams,
the most beautiful angel. Like steel
his victorious eyes were shining,
and the blood-red flames
of his torch lit up
my soul's deep vault.

"Will you come with me?" "No, never;
tombs and dead men frighten me."
But the iron hand
my right hand fiercely gripped.

"You will come with me." . . . And I advanced in my dream,
blinded by the red light.
And in the vault I heard the sounding chains,
and the stirring of caged beasts.

LXIV

From the threshold of a dream I was called . . .
It was the good voice, the beloved voice.

"Tell me: will you come with me to see the soul?"
A caress touched my heart.

"With you always." . . . And I advanced in my dream
through a long, bare gallery,
feeling the light touch of her pure robe
and the gentle pulse of her loving hand.

189

LXV
(Sueño infantil)

Una clara noche
de fiesta y de luna,
noche de mis sueños,
noche de alegría

—era luz mi alma
que hoy es bruma toda,
no eran mis cabellos
negros todavía—,

el hada más joven
me llevó en sus brazos
a la alegre fiesta
que en la plaza ardía.

So el chisporroteo
de las luminarias,
amor sus madejas
de danzas tejía.

Y en aquella noche
de fiesta y de luna,
noche de mis sueños,
noche de alegría,

el hada más joven
besaba mi frente . . .,
con su linda mano
su adiós me decía . . .

Todos los rosales
daban sus aromas,
todos los amores
amor entreabría.

190

LXV
(Childhood Dream)

One clear night
of fiesta and moon,
night of my dreams,
night of joy

—luminous was my soul,
which today is all mist,
and not yet black
was my hair—,

the youngest fairy
carried me in her arms
to the joyful fiesta
ablaze in the plaza.

Under the sparkling
of the festive lamps,
love its tangle
of dances was weaving.

And on that night
of fiesta and moon,
night of my dreams,
night of joy,

the youngest fairy
my forehead kissed . . .,
with her pretty hand
she gave me her goodbye . . .

All of the rosebushes
gave forth their aromas,
to all loves, love
half-opened the door.

191

LXVI

¡Y esos niños en hilera,
llevando el sol de la tarde
en sus velitas de cera! . . .

＊

¡De amarillo calabaza,
en el azul, cómo sube
la luna, sobre la plaza!

＊

Duro ceño.
Pirata, rubio africano,
barbitaheño.

＊

Lleva un alfanje en la mano.
Estas figuras del sueño . . .

＊

Donde las niñas cantan en corro,
en los jardines del limonar,
sobre la fuente, negro abejorro
pasa volando, zumba al volar.

Se oyó su bronco gruñir de abuelo
entre las claras voces sonar,
superflua nota de violoncelo
en los jardines del limonar.

LXVI

And those children in a row,
carrying the afternoon sun
in their little wax candles! . . .

✺

Of pumpkin yellow,
in the blue, how the moon
climbs above the plaza!

✺

Harsh frown.
Pirate, blond African
with a red beard.

✺

He carries a cutlass in his hand.
These dreamlike figures . . .

✺

Where the little girls sing in a circle,
in the gardens of the lemon grove,
over the fountain, a black bumblebee
flies by, buzzing as it goes.

Its* gruff grandfather growl was heard
to sound among the clear voices,
a superfluous cello note
in the gardens of the lemon grove.

*From the popular Austral editions of Espasa-Calpe to the more authoritative editions
of Geoffrey Ribbans, and Aurora de Albornoz and Guillermo de Torre (Antonio Ma-
chado, *Obras: Poesía y prosa*, Buenos Aires, Losada, 1964), *un* (a) has come to

Entre las cuatro blancas paredes,
cuando una mano cerró el balcón,
por los salones de sal-si-puedes
suena el rebato de su bordón.

. Muda en el techo, quieta, ¿dormida?
la negra nota de angustia está,
y en la pradera verdiflorida
de un sueño niño volando va . . .

Between the four white walls,
when a hand closed the window,
through the parlors of come-out-if-you-can
sounds the alarm of its base string.

Mute on the roof, motionless, asleep?
is the black note of anguish,
and in the green flowery meadow
of a childhood dream it goes flying by.

replace *su* (its) in this verse. But *su* makes more sense, because it shows that the "gruff grandfather growl" belongs to the bumblebee and *su* appears in Machado's *Poesías completas* of 1936 and in the well-known Mexican edition of Machado's *Obras* (Seneca, 1940).

LXVII

Si yo fuera un poeta
galante, cantaría
a vuestros ojos un cantar tan puro
como en el mármol blanco el agua limpia.

Y en una estrofa de agua
todo el cantar sería:

"Ya sé que no responden a mis ojos,
que ven y no preguntan cuando miran,
los vuestros claros; vuestros ojos tienen
la buena luz tranquila,
la buena luz del mundo en flor, que he visto
desde los brazos de mi madre un día."

LXVIII

Llamó a mi corazón, un claro día,
con un perfume de jazmín, el viento.

—A cambio de este aroma,
todo el aroma de tus rosas quiero.

—No tengo rosas; flores
en mi jardín no hay ya: todas han muerto.

Me llevaré los llantos de las fuentes,
las hojas amarillas y los mustios pétalos.
Y el viento huyó . . . Mi corazón sangraba . . .
Alma, ¿qué has hecho de tu pobre huerto?

LXVII

If I were a poet
of love, I would sing
to your eyes a song as pure
as clean water on white marble.

And in a stanza of water
the whole song would be:

"I now know that to my eyes, which see
and do not inquire when they look,
your clear eyes do not respond;
your eyes have the good tranquil light,
the good light of the world in bloom,
which one day from my mother's arms I saw."

LXVIII

One bright day, the wind called
to my heart with perfume of jasmine.

"In return for this aroma,
I want all the aroma of your roses."

"I have no roses; in my garden
are flowers no longer: all have died."

"I will carry off the tears of the fountains,
the yellow leaves and the faded petals."
And the wind fled . . . My heart bled . . .
"Soul, what have you done to your poor garden?"

197

LXIX

Hoy buscarás en vano
a tu dolor consuelo.

Lleváronse tus hadas
el lino de tus sueños.
Está la fuente muda,
y está marchito el huerto.
Hoy sólo quedan lágrimas
para llorar. No hay que llorar, ¡silencio!

LXX

Y nada importa ya que el vino de oro
rebose de tu copa cristalina,
o el agrio zumo enturbie el puro vaso . . .

Tú sabes las secretas galerías
del alma, los caminos de los sueños,
y la tarde tranquila
donde van a morir . . . Allí te aguardan

las hadas silenciosas de la vida,
y hacia un jardín de eterna primavera
te llevarán un día.

LXIX

Today you will seek in vain
consolation for your sorrow.

Your fairies have carried off
the flax of your dreams.
The fountain is mute,
and the garden withered.
Today only tears remain
to be shed. It's no use crying, silence!

LXX

And it no longer matters that the golden wine
should overflow your crystal goblet,
or the bitter juice becloud the pure glass . . .

You know the secret galleries
of the soul, the paths to dreams,
and the tranquil evening
where they go to die . . . There the silent

fairies of life await you,
and toward a garden of eternal spring
will they one day lead you.

LXXI

¡Tocados de otros días,
mustios encajes y marchitas sedas;
salterios arrumbados,
rincones de salas polvorientas;

daguerrotipos turbios,
cartas que amarillean;
libracos no leídos
que guardan grises florecitas secas:

romanticismos muertos,
cursilerías viejas,
cosas de ayer que sois el alma, y cantos
y cuentos de la abuela! . . .

LXXII

La casa tan querida
donde habitaba ella,
sobre un montón de escombros arruinada
o derruída, enseña
el negro y carcomido
maltrabado esqueleto de madera.

La luna está vertiendo
su clara luz en sueños que platea
en las ventanas. Mal vestido y triste,
voy caminando por la calle vieja.

LXXI

Headdresses of other days,
withered laces and faded silks;
discarded psalters,
corners of dusty parlors;

cloudy daguerreotypes,
letters turning yellow;
unread old books
holding little dry gray flowers:

romantic notions long dead,
old vulgarities,
yesterday's things that are the soul,
and grandmother's songs and tales! . . .

LXXII

The beloved house
where she dwelt,
ruined or demolished
upon a heap of rubble,
shows its black and worm-eaten
badly joined skeleton of wood.

The moon is pouring down
its bright dreamy light turning
to silver on the windows. Shabby and sad,
I make my way along the old street.

LXXIII

Ante el pálido lienzo de la tarde,
la iglesia, con sus torres afiladas
y el ancho campanario, en cuyos huecos
voltean suavemente las campanas,
alta y sombría, surge.

La estrella es una lágrima
en el azul celeste.
Bajo la estrella clara,
flota, vellón disperso,
una nube quimérica de plata.

LXXIV

Tarde tranquila, casi
con placidez de alma,
para ser joven, para haberlo sido
cuando Dios quiso, para
tener algunas alegrías . . . lejos,
y poder dulcemente recordarlas.

LXXIII

Before the evening's pale canvas
rises the church, tall and somber,
with its pointed tower and broad belfry,
in whose recesses the bells
softly peal.

The star is a teardrop
in the heavenly blue.
Under the bright star,
like a wisp of down,
floats a phantom silvery cloud.

LXXIV

A tranquil afternoon, almost
with serenity of soul,
to be young in, to have been so
when God willed it, to have
a few joys . . . far away,
and to be able sweetly to recall them.

LXXV

Yo, como Anacreonte,
quiero cantar, reír y echar al viento
las sabias amarguras
y los graves consejos,

y quiero, sobre todo, emborracharme,
ya lo sabéis . . . ¡Grotesco!
Pura fe en el morir, pobre alegría
y macabro danzar antes de tiempo.

LXXVI

¡Oh tarde luminosa!
El aire está encantado.
La blanca cigüeña
dormita volando,
y las golondrinas se cruzan, tendidas
las alas agudas al viento dorado,
y en la tarde risueña se alejan
volando, soñando . . .

Y hay una que torna como la saeta,
las alas agudas tendidas al aire sombrío,
buscando su negro rincón del tejado.

La blanca cigüeña,
como un garabato,
tranquila y disforme ¡tan disparatada!
sobre el campanario.

LXXV

Like Anacreon, I wish
to sing, laugh and cast to the wind
wise bitter thoughts
and solemn advice,

and I wish, above all, to get drunk,
now you know . . . Grotesque!
Pure faith in dying, poor joy
and macabre dancing before my time.

LXXVI

Oh luminous afternoon!
The air is enchanted.
The white stork
dozes in flight, and
the swallows crisscross, their sharp wings
extended on the golden wind,
and in the smiling afternoon
dreaming they fly away . . .

And there is one that returns like an arrow,
its wings extended on the somber air,
seeking its black corner of the tiled roof.

The white stork,
like a pothook,
tranquil and ill-shaped, so absurd!
on the belfry.

LXXVII

Es una tarde cenicienta y mustia,
destartalada, como el alma mía;
y es esta vieja angustia
que habita mi usual hipocondría.

La causa de esta angustia no consigo
ni vagamente comprender siquiera;
pero recuerdo y, recordando, digo:
—Sí, yo era niño, y tú, mi compañera.

✳

Y no es verdad, dolor, yo te conozco,
tú eres nostalgia de la vida buena
y soledad de corazón sombrío,
de barco sin naufragio y sin estrella.

Como perro olvidado que no tiene
huella ni olfato y yerra
por los caminos, sin camino, como
el niño que en la noche de una fiesta

se pierde entre el gentío
y el aire polvoriento y las candelas
chispeantes, atónito, y asombra
su corazón de música y de pena,

así voy yo, borracho melancólico,
guitarrista lunático, poeta,
y pobre hombre en sueños,
siempre buscando a Dios entre la niebla.

LXXVII

It is an ashen and gloomy afternoon,
untidy, like my soul;
and it's this old anguish
that inhabits my usual hypochondria.

The cause of this anguish I cannot
even vaguely understand;
but I remember, and remembering, I say:
"Yes, I was a little boy, and you, my sweet companion."

✳

And it's not true, sorrow, I know you,
you are nostalgia for the good life
and loneliness of a somber heart,
of a vessel without shipwreck or star.

Like an abandoned dog that has
neither track nor scent and wanders
the ways without a way, like
a child who on a night of fiesta

gets lost among the throng
and the dusty air and the sparkling
candles, astonished, and his heart
grows dark with music and grief,

so go I, melancholy tippler,
moonstruck guitarist, poet,
and poor devil in dreams,
ever searching for God in the mist.

LXXVIII

    ¿Y ha de morir contigo el mundo mago
donde guarda el recuerdo
los hálitos más puros de la vida,
la blanca sombra del amor primero,

    la voz que fue a tu corazón, la mano
que tú querías retener en sueños,
y todos los amores
que llegaron al alma, al hondo cielo?

    ¿Y ha de morir contigo el mundo tuyo,
la vieja vida en orden tuyo y nuevo?
¿Los yunques y crisoles de tu alma
trabajan para el polvo y para el viento?

LXXIX

    Desnuda está la tierra,
y el alma aúlla al horizonte pálido
como loba famélica. ¿Que buscas,
poeta, en el ocaso?

    Amargo caminar, porque el camino
pesa en el corazón. ¡El viento helado,
y la noche que llega, y la amargura
de la distancia! . . . En el camino blanco

    algunos yertos árboles negrean;
en los montes lejanos
hay oro y sangre . . . El sol murió . . . ¿Qué buscas,
poeta, en el ocaso?

LXXVIII

And must it die with you, the magic
world where memory keeps
the purest breaths of life,
the white shadow of the first love,

the voice that reached your heart,
the hand you wished to hold in dreams,
and all the loves
that touched the soul, the deep heaven?

And must your world die with you,
the old life newly formed by you?
Do the anvils and crucibles of your soul
work for the dust and the wind?

LXXIX

Naked is the land,
and the soul howls at the pale horizon
like a hungry she-wolf. What do you
seek, O poet, in the sunset?

Bitter wayfaring, because the way
lies heavy on the heart. The icy wind,
the approaching night, and the bitterness
of the distance! . . . On the white road

some rigid trees turn black;
on the faraway mountains
there is gold and blood . . . The sun has died . . .
What do you seek, O poet, in the sunset?

LXXX
(Campo)

La tarde está muriendo
como un hogar humilde que se apaga.

Allá, sobre los montes,
quedan algunas brasas.

Y ese árbol roto en el camino blanco
hace llorar de lástima.

¡Dos ramas en el tronco herido, y una
hoja marchita y negra en cada rama!

¿Lloras? . . . Entre los álamos de oro,
lejos, la sombra del amor te aguarda.

LXXX
(Countryside)

The afternoon is dying
like a humble hearth that's going out.

Far away, above the mountains,
a few live coals remain.

And that broken tree on the white road
makes one cry with pity.

Two branches on the wounded trunk, and
one black and withered leaf on each branch!

Do you weep? . . . Among the golden poplars,
far away, the shadow of love awaits you.

LXXXI

(A un viejo y distinguido señor)

Te he visto, por el parque ceniciento
que los poetas aman
para llorar, como una noble sombra
vagar, envuelto en tu levita larga.

El talante cortés, ha tantos años
compuesto de una fiesta en la antesala,
¡qué bien tus pobres huesos
ceremoniosos guardan!

Yo te he visto, aspirando distraído,
con el aliento que la tierra exhala
—hoy, tibia tarde en que las mustias hojas
húmedo viento arranca—,
del eucalipto verde

el frescor de las hojas perfumadas.
Y te he visto llevar la seca mano
a la perla que brilla en tu corbata.

LXXXI
(To an Old and Distinguished Gentleman)

Wrapped in your long frock coat,
I have seen you, like a noble shadow,
wander about the ash-tinged park
where poets love to weep.

Your courteous bearing composed
so many years ago on the threshold of a fiesta,
how well your poor ceremonious
bones sustain it!

I have seen you inhaling, distracted
by the breath the earth gives off
—today, mild afternoon on which
a damp wind tears off the faded leaves—

the freshness of the scented leaves
of the green eucalyptus tree.
And I have seen you raise your thin hand
to the pearl that on your necktie shines.

213

LXXXII

(Los sueños)

El hada más hermosa ha sonreído
al ver la lumbre de una estrella pálida,
que en hilo suave, blanco y silencioso
se enrosca al huso de su rubia hermana.

Y vuelve a sonreír, porque en su rueca
el hilo de los campos se enmaraña.
Tras la tenue cortina de la alcoba
está el jardín envuelto en luz dorada.

La cuna, casi en sombra. El niño duerme.
Dos hadas laboriosas lo acompañan,
hilando de los sueños los sutiles
copos en ruecas de marfil y plata.

LXXXIII

Guitarra del mesón que hoy suenas jota,
mañana petenera,
según quien llega y tañe
las empolvadas cuerdas,

guitarra del mesón de los caminos,
no fuiste nunca, ni serás, poeta.

Tú eres alma que dice su armonía
solitaria a las almas pasajeras . . .

Y siempre que te escucha el caminante
sueña escuchar un aire de su tierra.

LXXXII
(Dreams)

The most beautiful fairy smiled
on seeing the light of a pale star
coiling in soft, white, silent thread
around the spindle of her fair-haired sister.

And she smiles again, for on her distaff
the thread of the fields becomes entangled.
Behind the thin curtain of the bedroom
the garden is enveloped in golden light.

The cradle, almost in shadow. The child sleeps.
Two industrious fairies keep him company,
spinning the delicate tufts of dreams
on distaffs of ivory and silver.

LXXXIII

O guitar of the inn, today you sound
one tune, tomorrow another,*
depending on who arrives and plucks
your dusty strings,

guitar of the roadside inn,
poet you never were, nor ever will be.

You are a soul that speaks its lonely
harmony to transient souls . . .

And whenever the traveler hears you,
he dreams he's listening to a native air.

* *Jotas* and *petenera* are untranslatable. The first is a well-known folk tune and dance
of Aragon, Navarre, and parts of Levant; the second is an Andalusian folk tune.

LXXXIV

El rojo sol de un sueño en el Oriente asoma.
Luz en sueños. ¿No tiemblas, andante peregrino?
Pasado el llano verde, en la florida loma,
acaso está el cercano final de tu camino.

Tú no verás del trigo la espiga sazonada
y de macizas pomas cargado el manzanar,
ni de la vid rugosa la uva aurirrosada
ha de exprimir su alegre licor en tu lagar.

Cuando el primer aroma exhalen los jazmines
y cuando más palpiten las rosas del amor,
una mañana de oro que alumbre los jardines,
¿no huirá, como una nube dispersa, el sueño en flor?

Campo recién florido y verde, ¡quién pudiera
soñar aún largo tiempo en esas pequeñitas
corolas azuladas que manchan la pradera,
y en esas diminutas primeras margaritas!

LXXXIV

The red sun of a dream appears in the East.
Light in dreams. Do you not tremble, roving pilgrim?
Beyond the green plain, on the flowering hill,
the end of your journey is perhaps at hand.

You will not see the ripened ear of wheat
and the apple orchard laden with firm apples,
nor will the golden-pink grape of the wrinkled vine
release its merry liquor in your wine press.

When the jasmine sends forth its first aroma
and love's roses tremble most, and
a golden morning lights up the gardens,
will the flowery dream not flee like a scattered cloud?

O countryside just flowered and green, would
that I might still long dream of those little
blue corollas that dot the meadow,
and of those tiny first daisies!

LXXXV

La primavera besaba
suavemente la arboleda,
y el verde nuevo brotaba
como una verde humareda.

Las nubes iban pasando
sobre el campo juvenil . . .
Yo vi en las hojas temblando
las frescas lluvias de abril.

Bajo ese almendro florido,
todo cargado de flor,
—recordé—, yo he maldecido
mi juventud sin amor.

Hoy, en mitad de la vida,
me he parado a meditar . . .
¡Juventud nunca vivida,
quién te volviera a soñar!

LXXXV

Spring softly kissed
the grove of trees,
and the new green came out
like a cloud of green smoke.

The clouds were passing
over the youthful countryside . . .
On the leaves I saw the fresh
rains of April trembling.

Under that almond tree in flower,
all laden with blossoms,
—I remembered—, I cursed
my loveless youth.

Today, midway in life,
I have paused to meditate . . .
O never-lived youthful days,
if only I might dream you again!

LXXXVI

Eran ayer mis dolores
como gusanos de seda
que iban labrando capullos;
hoy son mariposas negras.

¡De cuántas flores amargas
he sacado blanca cera!
¡Oh, tiempo en que mis pesares
trabajaban como abejas!

Hoy son como avenas locas,
o cizaña en sementera,
como tizón en espiga,
como carcoma en madera.

¡Oh, tiempo en que mis dolores
tenían lágrimas buenas,
y eran como agua de noria
que va regando una huerta!
Hoy son agua de torrente
que arranca el limo a la tierra.

Dolores que ayer hicieron
de mi corazón colmena,
hoy tratan mi corazón
como a una muralla vieja:
quieren derribarlo, y pronto,
al golpe de la piqueta.

LXXXVI

Yesterday my sorrows
were like silkworms
fashioning cocoons;
today they are black moths.

From how many bitter flowers
have I drawn white wax!
Oh, time when my griefs
were wont to work like bees!

Today they are like wild oats,
like darnel in sown fields,
like black smut on spikes of wheat,
like deathwatch beetles in wood.

Oh, time when my sorrows
had good tears,
and were like a noria
watering a garden!
Today they are flood water
stripping the topsoil from the land.

Sorrows that yesterday made
a beehive out of my heart,
today treat my heart
like an old wall:
they want to knock it down, and soon,
under the blows of a pickax.

LXXXVII
(Renacimiento)

Galerías del alma . . . ¡El alma niña!
Su clara luz risueña;
y la pequeña historia,
y la alegría de la vida nueva . . .

¡Ah, volver a nacer, y andar camino,
ya recobrada la perdida senda!

Y volver a sentir en nuestra mano
aquel latido de la mano buena
de nuestra madre . . . Y caminar en sueños
por amor de la mano que nos lleva.

＊

En nuestras almas todo
por misteriosa mano se gobierna.
Incomprensibles, mudas,
nada sabemos de las almas nuestras.

Las más hondas palabras
del sabio nos enseñan
lo que el silbar del viento cuando sopla,
o el sonar de las aguas cuando ruedan.

LXXXVII
(Rebirth)

Galleries of the soul . . . The child's soul!
Its bright smiling light;
and its brief history,
and the joy of new life . . .

Ah, to be born again and walk along,
the lost path once more regained!

And to feel again in our hand
that heartbeat of our mother's
kind hand . . . And to walk in a dream
for love of the hand that leads us.

❋

In our souls everything
by a mysterious hand is governed.
Of our unfathomable, silent
souls, we know nothing at all.

The profoundest words
of the wise man teach us
what the whistling wind when it blows
or the sounding of rolling waters.

LXXXVIII

Tal vez la mano, en sueños,
del sembrador de estrellas,
hizo sonar la música olvidada

como una nota de la lira inmensa,
y la ola humilde a nuestros labios vino
de unas pocas palabras verdaderas.

LXXXIX

Y podrás conocerte, recordando
del pasado soñar los turbios lienzos,
en este día triste en que caminas
con los ojos abiertos.

De toda la memoria, sólo vale
el don preclaro de evocar los sueños.

XC

Los árboles conservan
verdes aún las copas,
pero del verde mustio
de las marchitas frondas.

El agua de la fuente,
sobre la piedra tosca
y de verdín cubierta,
resbala silenciosa.

Arrastra el viento algunas
amarillentas hojas.
¡El viento de la tarde
sobre la tierra en sombra!

LXXXVIII

Perhaps, in a dream, the hand
of the sower of stars
made the forgotten music sound

like a note of the immense lyre,
and to our lips came the humble wave
of a few truthful words.

LXXXIX

And you'll be able to know yourself
by recalling the dim canvases of past dreaming
on this sad day when you walk
with your eyes wide open.

Of all memory, only the illustrious gift
of evoking dreams has value.

XC

The trees still retain
the green of their tops,
but the faded green
of withered foliage.

The water of the fountain
slips silently over
the rough stone
covered with green moss.

The wind carries off
some yellowish leaves.
The wind of evening
over the shadowy land!

XCI

Húmedo está, bajo el laurel, el banco
de verdinosa piedra;
lavó la lluvia, sobre el muro blanco,
las empolvadas hojas de la hiedra.

Del viento del otoño el tibio aliento
los céspedes undula, y la alameda
conversa con el viento . . .
¡el viento de la tarde en la arboleda!

Mientras el sol en el ocaso esplende
que los racimos de la vid orea,
y el buen burgués, en su balcón, enciende
la estoica pipa en que el tabaco humea,

voy recordando versos juveniles . . .
¿Qué fue de aquel mi corazón sonoro?
¿Será cierto que os vais, sombras gentiles,
huyendo entre los árboles de oro?

XCI

Under the laurel tree, the bench
of greenish stone is damp;
the rain has washed, on the white wall,
the ivy's dusty leaves.

The mild breath of autumn wind
waves the grass, and the poplar grove
converses with the wind . . .
the afternoon wind among the trees!

While the sun splendors in the West,
the sun that nourishes the clusters of grapes,
and on his balcony the good burgher lights
the stoical pipe where the tobacco smokes,

I am remembering youthful verses . . .
What happened to that sonorous heart of mine?
Can it be true, graceful shades, that
you depart, fleeing among the golden trees?

VARIA ✳ VARIA

XCII

Tournez, tournez, chevaux de bois.—Verlaine

Pegasos, lindos pegasos,
caballitos de madera.

. . . .

Yo conocí, siendo niño,
la alegría de dar vueltas
sobre un corcel colorado,
en una noche de fiesta.

En el aire polvoriento
chispeaban las candelas,
y la noche azul ardía
toda sembrada de estrellas.

¡Alegrías infantiles
que cuestan una moneda
de cobre, lindos pegasos,
caballitos de madera!

230

XCII

Tournez, tournez, chevaux de bois.—Verlaine

Like Pegasus, pretty Pegasus,
little horses of wood.

. . . .

As a child, I knew
the joy of circling round
and round upon a colored steed
on a night of fiesta.

In the dusty air
the candles were sparkling
and the blue night blazed,
all sown with stars.

Childish joys
costing a copper coin,
like pretty Pegasus,
little horses of wood.

XCIII

Deletreos de armonía
que ensaya inexperta mano.

Hastío. Cacofonía
del sempiterno piano
que yo de niño escuchaba
soñando . . . no sé con qué,

con algo que no llegaba,
todo lo que se fue.

XCIV

En medio de la plaza y sobre tosca piedra,
el agua brota y brota. En el cercano huerto,
eleva, tras el muro ceñido por la hiedra,
alto ciprés la mancha de su ramaje yerto.

La tarde está cayendo frente a los caserones
de la ancha plaza, en sueños. Relucen las vidrieras
con ecos mortecinos de sol. En los balcones
hay formas que parecen confusas calaveras.

La calma es infinita en la desierta plaza,
donde pasea el alma su traza de alma en pena.
El agua brota y brota en la marmórea taza.
En todo el aire en sombra no más que el agua suena.

XCIII

Spellings of harmony
rehearsed by an untutored hand.

Boredom. Cacophony
of the everlasting piano
I listened to as a child
adreaming . . . I don't know of what,

of something that didn't quite arrive,
all that has now gone away.

XCIV

In the middle of the plaza and on rough stone,
the water surges and surges. In the nearby garden,
behind the ivy-clad wall, a lofty
cypress lifts its patch of rigid branches.

Evening falls opposite the big houses
in the wide dreaming plaza. The balcony windows
glitter with the dying echoes of the sun. On the balconies
are forms that look like vague skulls.

Calm is infinite in the deserted plaza,
where the soul parades its air of soul in purgatory.
The water surges and surges in the marble basin.
In the whole shadowy air only the water sounds.

XCV
(Coplas mundanas)

Poeta ayer, hoy triste y pobre
filósofo trasnochado,
tengo en monedas de cobre
el oro de ayer cambiado.

Sin placer y sin fortuna,
pasó como una quimera
mi juventud, la primera . . .
la sola, no hay más que una:
la de dentro es la de fuera.

Pasó como un torbellino,
bohemia y aborrascada,
harta de copas y vino,
mi juventud bien amada.

Y hoy miro a las galerías
del recuerdo, para hacer
aleluyas de elegías
desconsoladas de ayer.

¡Adiós, lágrimas cantoras,
lágrimas que alegremente
brotabais, como en la fuente
las limpias aguas sonoras!

¡Buenas lágrimas vertidas
por un amor juvenil,
cual frescas lluvias caídas
sobre los campos de abril!

No canta ya el ruiseñor
de cierta noche serena;

XCV
(Mundane Verses)

Yesterday a poet, today a sad,
poor, time-worn philosopher,
my yesterday's gold
to copper coins has turned.

Without pleasure and without fortune,
my youth, my first and only
youth, there is but one:
the one within is the one without,
like a phantom passed by.

It passed like a whirlwind,
bohemian and tempestuous,
sated with verse and wine,
my beloved youth.

And today I look toward the galleries
of memory to make doggerel
out of yesterday's
disconsolate elegies.

Goodbye, singing tears,
tears that flowed as happily
as the clear sonorous
waters in the fountain.

Good tears shed
for a youthful love,
like fresh rains fallen
on April's fields.

No longer sings the nightingale
of a certain night serene;

sanamos del mal de amor
que sabe llorar sin pena.

Poeta ayer, hoy triste y pobre
filósofo trasnochado,
tengo en monedas de cobre
el oro de ayer cambiado.

XCVI
(Sol de invierno)

Es mediodía. Un parque.
Invierno. Blancas sendas;
simétricos montículos
y ramas esqueléticas.

Bajo el invernadero,
naranjos en maceta,
y en su tonel, pintado
de verde, la palmera.

Un viejecillo dice,
para su capa vieja:
"¡El sol, esta hermosura
de sol! . . ." Los niños juegan.

El agua de la fuente
resbala, corre y sueña
lamiendo, casi muda,
la verdinosa piedra.

we've gotten over the love
sickness that weeps without grief.

Yesterday a poet, today a sad,
poor, time-worn philosopher,
my yesterday's gold
to copper coins has turned.

XCVI
(Winter Sun)

It is noon. A park.
Winter. White paths;
symmetrical little mounds
and skeletal branches.

Under the hothouse roof,
orange trees in pots,
and in its barrel, painted
green, the palm tree.

A little old man says
to his old cape:
"The sunshine, this beautiful
sunshine! . . ." The children play.

The water in the fountain
glides, runs and dreams
licking, almost silent,
the greenish stone.